Too Blessed to Be Stressed

Too Blessed to Be Stressed

DR. SUZAN D. JOHNSON COOK

THOMAS NELSON PUBLISHERS
Nashville
Printed in the United States of America

Published in Nashville, Tennessee, by Thomas Nelson, Inc., Publishers.

Unless otherwise noted, Scripture quotations are from THE NEW KING JAMES VERSION, Copyright © 1979, 1980, 1982, 1990, Thomas Nelson, Inc., Publishers.

Scripture quotations noted KJV are from the KING JAMES VERSION.

Scripture quotations noted NIV are from the HOLY BIBLE: NEW INTERNATIONAL VERSION, Copyright © 1973, 1978, 1984 by International Bible Society. Used by permission of Zondervan Publishing House. All rights reserved.

Library of Congress Cataloging-in-Publication Data

Johnson Cook, Suzan D. (Suzan Denise), 1957–
    Too blessed to be stressed : words of wisdom for women on the move.
        p. cm.
    ISBN 0-7852-7070-1
    1. Women—Religious life.   2. Stress (Psychology)—Religious aspects—Christianity.   3. Johnson Cook, Suzan D. (Suzan Denise), 1957– . I. Title.
BV4527.J65   1998
248.8'43—DC21   97–45839
                                                                      CIP

1 2 3 4 5 6 QPK 03 02 01 00 99 98
Printed in the United States of America

Dedication

To the many women who have blessed my life, especially

my sister-friends:
Nina, Darnita, Linda, Yoki, Alexis, Cora,
Sonnie, Naomi, Mae, and Carol

my seven daughters in ministry:
Sheila, Henrietta, Carolyn, Valerie,
Gladys, Leatha, and Annette

my prayer partners:
Melody and Mercedes

my church sisters from Rendall Memorial Presbyterian,
Union Baptist, Mariners' Temple Baptist,
and Bronx Christian Fellowship

my family:
Mom, Jessica, Tina, Lucille, Louise,
Lydia, Bertha, and Jackie

Theresa, who cares for my children when I am on the move,

and to the loving memory of Mama, Bee, and Katherine

Contents

Acknowledgments   *ix*

Chapter 1   Too Blessed to Be Stressed   *1*

Chapter 2   Know Whose You Are   *17*

Chapter 3   Know Who You Are   *31* 25 Joy

Chapter 4   Know Where You're Going   *47*

Chapter 5   Know When to Leave   *63*

Chapter 6   Go Forward   *85*

Chapter 7   Go with the Flow   *105*

Chapter 8   Live Abundantly   *123*

Chapter 9   Live Victoriously   *133*

Chapter 10   Don't Block Your Blessing   *147*

Chapter 11   Sisterstrength   *161*

Notes   *177*

About the Author   *178*

Acknowledgments

First and foremost, I praise God for the wonderful journey of life and ministry I have had.

There are many to whom I give thanks. My parents, Dorothy and the late Wilbert T. Johnson, were Christians, visionaries, community activists, and agents of love who prepared me for and shared me with the world. It has been a long way from living in a walk-up tenement apartment on Harlem's 144th Street to flying on *Air Force One* as an advisor to the president of the United States. To God be the glory!

Because my parents often shared our home with others, I have learned to share what I have, including my faith stories and life's lessons. This book is a sharing experience and a testament of faith as I continue to evolve into the woman God would have me to be.

I am amazed how God brings the right people together at the right time. Truly there are matches made in heaven; I am a living witness. So I send much love to the men in my life, who love me unconditionally as we build our family and a lasting legacy of love: my husband, Ron, my prayer partner and soul mate, who reminds me that it is all right to be the recipient of roses, but it is also important to take the time to smell them; and our two sons, Samuel David and Christopher Daniel, who remind me how pleasurable, honorable, and regal it is to be a mommy.

I cannot write any book without acknowledging the matriarchs and patriarchs of our family, the role models and foundation

Acknowledgments

builders who prayed for me and encouraged me at every juncture, who taught me to hold my ground while standing on Holy Ground, who admonished me to never compromise my faith or my heritage.

I certainly thank Thomas Nelson Publishers for giving these words a chance to "become flesh." My heartfelt appreciation is extended to Lois de la Haba, my literary agent, as well as Rolf Zettersten, Janet Thoma, Connie Reece, and all the wonderful people who advised and prayed with and for me through this process.

More love also goes out to the other men and women in my life: to my brother, Ronald, and Tina; to my only niece and nephew, Jessica and Charles Jr.; and to the "New Dream Team"— Mae and James Jones, Coral Aubert, Annette Cox, Sissy Peoples, Maharold Peoples, Willie Phipps, Grace Samuels, the Reverends Rodney Brooks and Ruth Ransom, Douglas Banks, and the entire Bronx Christian Fellowship family, who have allowed my gifts in ministry to soar without limits and who have helped my joy for ministry to return.

Finally, I offer a special thanksgiving to God for those in the Yankee Stadium area of the Bronx who have embraced me and welcomed me back home. I am remarkably blessed.

CHAPTER ONE

Too Blessed to
Be Stressed

'm Sujay, and I need an entire month off." The words tumbled out with a laugh.

In that awkward millisecond while my brain was processing what to say next, I scanned the room. A dozen women had gathered around a conference table in the library of the stately Convent Avenue Baptist Church. The group of sister ministers met monthly for encouragement and fellowship. With so few women in ministry, and even fewer black women, the peer group was invaluable.

Before I could come up with my next line, the moderator, a Christian counselor named Doris, spoke up. "Say that again, please."

Perhaps she didn't hear me, I thought. So I complied. "I'm Sujay, and I need an entire month off."

Doris had started the meeting by asking each woman to introduce herself and share something she needed in her ministry.

Usually we spoke about our accomplishments and goals, the successful sermons, the people we had helped. We were all new in our ministries and excited to have embarked on a great adventure with God.

But this day the conversation had taken an introspective turn. The two or three women who preceded me spoke of resources they lacked or advice they needed. They opened up about problems they were facing.

Not Suzan "Sujay" Johnson. When my turn came, I tried to make a joke out of it. Me? Admit a struggle? It wasn't in my nature. I was born with a winning attitude. When I reach for a star, I always manage to grab one. My dreams are bigger than I am—that's big because I'm almost six feet tall—and the word *defeat* is not in my vocabulary.

My attempt at humor bombed.

Doris wasn't laughing. "Say that again," she insisted.

Why is she singling me out to mess with me? I was aggravated, but I said it again: "I need an entire month off." And when I heard myself say it for the third time, it finally dawned on me that it wasn't funny at all. I really did need a month off.

In my early twenties, with tons of energy, I thought I could do it all—I thought I *had* to do it all. Somehow I had equated being a leader with making myself indispensable. So I worked seven days a week. And because I was single, I placed few boundaries on my private time or space; others placed no boundaries at all.

"Tell me more about it," Doris said.

"Well, I've just completed my first year of pastoring. I guess I really am tired. I haven't taken a vacation, but I really can't."

"What did you say you need, Sujay?"

"I said I need a month off. But . . ." I started making excuses.

"Take the month off," Doris said.

The others chimed in. "If you need a month, take a month."

I protested a while longer, but I had to admit I was exhausted. I had been working nonstop. All my hard work had paid off, though. Under my leadership, in just six months Mariners' Temple had grown from fifteen tired saints to more than 150 people of all ages who were enthusiastic about church and eager to hear God's Word.

Now, in spite of my success in ministry, I was depressed and irritated. No wonder. I had not taken the time my body needed to rest and recover. Somehow I thought vacations were for everyone else, and I could just hold on while they were off having fun, then I would preach about how they should take a vacation again when the time permitted.

I had not heard my own sermons. I celebrated my members' promotions, attended their appreciation banquets, advised them on their relocations, encouraged them to be good to themselves because they deserved it. "You've worked hard," I would say, "so go for it." Meanwhile, I had neglected myself and jeopardized my emotional and physical health.

I was stressed out and headed for burnout.

Women on the Move

I entered the ministry at a time when it was not popular for women to be leaders in the church. In many quarters, women leaders are still not accepted. I was the first African-American woman in my denomination elected as a senior pastor, and some of the male vanguard from many places were determined that would never happen. To merely say that doors were slammed in my face would not give you a true understanding of the challenges I faced. (I will share some of those challenges with you later.)

Finding my place in ministry was always stressful and at times distressing. Yet I had to deal with the challenges, for I truly believed God had called me to be an ordained minister. I had to learn how to live with stressful situations without becoming stressed out. That is one of the lessons I want to impart to you: *stress does not have to stress you out.*

3

One of my sister-friends recently visited her "energy therapist," who informed her that the reason for her stress was that her body was moving ahead of her "aura." I would simply say that she was moving too fast and her spirit could not catch up. That is my definition of stress: when body and spirit are not in the same place at the same time.

Blessings are gifts from God that allow us to align our bodies with our minds and souls. If we learn to walk in those blessings, to make them a way of life, then we will become too blessed to be stressed.

The church world has made it difficult for women to take a role in leadership, but society as a whole is still trying to make adjustments for women at any level of leadership in any arena. Those who are breaking the barriers in their fields have been through struggles similar to mine.

And professional women are not the only ones who are stressed out by demands that drain their time and energy. Virtually every woman I meet seems to be stressed out to some degree—the frazzled wife and mother trying to juggle a career and family life, the single mother holding down two minimum-wage jobs and struggling financially, the older woman facing an economic and emotional burden because her husband's job has been downsized, or the caregiver tending the needs of a chronically ill child or an elderly parent.

Stress is no respecter of persons. It does not discriminate. It hits everyone. Stress transcends all lifestyles, ages, races, and classes.

But I have good news. Although we cannot avoid stress, we do not have to be distressed. We do not have to let stress conquer us. We can find the strength and power we need for life's journey.

I recently opened a new church. One of the myriad details that had to be taken care of was having the electricity connected. When I made arrangements with our local utility company, a representative set an appointment to come out to the premises and turn the power on. Because the building had previously had electric service, all he really did was give us access; the power was already there, even though we couldn't see it. The utility company gave us the ability to connect with and tap into that power source.

As Christians, we, too, have an invisible resource available. All we have to do is get connected to the power supply. It's already there—just make the connection and bust the stress!

Jesus Has Got the Juice

How do you make the connection? The Holy Spirit is your invisible power supply, and the one who can give you access to the power—the one who can get you connected—is Jesus Christ.

I like to say it this way: Jesus has got the juice.

In urban culture, *juice* is a popular term that expresses power and authority. By worldly measures, it's important for folks to know just who's got the juice. People spend a lot of time talking about it, trying to get it, or claiming they've already got it.

I worked in television in my first career, and we engaged in a constant battle over who had the juice. Was it the producer, the director, the on-air talent, the people who sold commercials? Just who had the juice? It became a cutthroat industry because everybody was trying to get the juice.

Then I went to Harvard and entered the academic world. Harvard is one of the world's great universities, but the people there were also battling over who had the juice. Was it the tenured professors, the ones with Ph.D.'s, or the nontenured professors? Was it the adjunct faculty or the students? The whole time I was there, people were fussing and fighting over who really had the juice.

And then I went to Washington, to the White House, the place known as the seat of power in our country. Lord, have mercy! Everybody was trying to get close to those who were close to the president. For an entire year I watched folks jockeying for position because they wanted to be next to the one they thought had the juice.

Even in the church world, there is a constant demand for clarification about who's got the juice. Who's in charge? Is it the preacher? The deacons? Those who were once on fire for the Lord get into arguments, and then when they feel they've got the juice, they lose their flame. I tell my church, "Don't let the ones with the juice get loose!"

Let's look at what the Bible says about it. Jesus told his disciples, the ones who would have responsibility for building the church and carrying out the Great Commission, "All authority [or power] has been given to Me in heaven and on earth" (Matt. 28:18).

All authority. *All* power. Jesus has got the juice.

The world's juice is temporary. It's good as long as you've got some money. It's good as long as you look good. But you can go broke and burn yourself out trying to get the world's juice. And when you get it, it won't last.

If you want real juice in your life, hook up with the Juice Maker. Get so close to Jesus that you become juicy with fruit— love, joy, peace, patience, kindness, goodness, faithfulness, gentleness, and self-control (Gal. 5:22–23).

Draw close to Christ. Believe that God *is*, and that he rewards those who diligently seek him (Heb. 11:6). God desires spiritual intimacy with you. You can never be too close to God. You may stray far away sometimes, but you can never be too close.

Do you know the old hymn that says, "Draw me nearer, Lord"? I love to sing the hymns of the church, and I've learned many spiritual lessons through music. I can't sing these old songs for you, of course, but I've interspersed some of them in these pages, along with a little nugget of wisdom. If you have a church background similar to mine, you'll know most of the songs. As you encounter them, why not pause and enjoy singing as a devotional exercise? If you're not familiar with a hymn, just read the words—out loud if you're in a private spot—and let the Spirit put the melody in your heart.

I Am Thine, O Lord

I am Thine, O Lord, I have heard Thy voice,
And it told Thy love to me;
But I long to rise in the arms of faith,
And be closer drawn to Thee.

Chorus:
Draw me nearer, nearer, blessed Lord,
To the cross where Thou hast died;
Draw me nearer, nearer, nearer, blessed Lord,
To Thy precious, bleeding side.

O the pure delight of a single hour
That before Thy throne I spend;
When I kneel in prayer, and with Thee, my God,
I commune as friend with friend!

Fanny Crosby, the most prolific gospel hymn writer in America, wrote these words in 1875. As a conversation with friends turned to the topic of enjoying God's presence and nearness, Fanny spontaneously spoke the lines of this poem. She lived so close to God that her heart continually overflowed with hymns of praise and, like this one, they often seemed to spring forth whole and complete.

You don't have to pray for hours to draw near to God. If you have only two minutes, take that time to commune with him and enjoy his presence.

Lord, Keep Me from Falling Apart

Jude recorded this wonderful thought: God is "able to keep you from falling" (Jude 24 NIV). I would like to add just one word to that verse: God is able to keep you from falling apart.

I became a mother for the first time at age thirty-four, just one week before my first wedding anniversary. Marriage was a big enough adjustment, but I was totally unprepared for motherhood—yet God kept me from falling apart through all the changes he had brought into my life.

My husband, Ron, and I had a storybook wedding. Because I am well known in New York City, and because we both come from sizable church families, it was a very large wedding. More than twenty-five hundred guests, including the mayor, the police commissioner, and many police officers (I serve as a chaplain for the New York City Police Department), joined us on October 11, 1991, at Riverside Church for the ceremony. We received the guests and cut our wedding cake at a large reception there at the church. Afterward, we had a private reception for about two hundred close friends and family at the historic Tavern on the Green, exactly as I had pictured it in my childhood dreams.

Tuxedoed groomsmen and dignitaries offered the customary toasts, their speeches accompanied by the joyful clinking of crystal. Then Ron and I spoke a few words, honoring our parents and thanking God for his blessing. As my parting shot I announced to the guests, "And we'll see you all at this time next year for our baby blessing." I was joking, as usual, but my words turned out to be prophetic.

I had always wanted a family, and Ron and I prayed about children from the beginning. God answered those prayers even sooner than we expected. He also answered our prayers for a safe delivery and a healthy baby. And on October 4, 1992, little Samuel, whose name means "gift of God," came kicking and crying into this world.

This new gift brought much joy, but it also changed my life—dramatically. I was so excited about giving birth, but somehow my brain had not grasped the fact that after the delivery there would be a lifelong process of raising a child. I thought having a baby was kind of like playing basketball: you toss it through the hoops, somebody gets the rebound, everybody cheers, and the game goes on.

Growing up, I was a tomboy and hooked on sports. (If the Women's National Basketball Association had been around in those days, the drive to play professionally might have competed with God's call to preach. But that's another story.) I didn't baby-sit frequently as some teenage girls do. Also, I was the younger of only two children in our family, so I wasn't around babies all that much. When I finally got around to having children of my own, no one sat me down and told me just how drastic and how stressful the changes in my lifestyle would be.

I was used to getting on and off airplanes at least twice a week, with no responsibility for anyone but myself. Suddenly another human being was completely dependent on me, and I couldn't even leave the apartment and take the elevator down to the mail-box without making arrangements for someone to watch him. And this tiny little creature could not tell me what he needed or wanted. He just cried, and I had to learn how to figure out what was wrong; more than that, I had to figure out what to do about it.

Perhaps the most startling revelation for this unprepared new mother was this: *poop happens.* And it happened with such frequency that I was appalled. Now, my husband is a gem. He has always shared responsibility for household duties, and he was wonderful with the baby. But in those first few weeks I pawned off so many dirty-diaper changes on Ron that he finally said, "Suzan, get over it. You are this baby's mother. You've got to learn to deal with poop!"

Another thing nobody told me was that you need to have Plan B ready for your Sunday wardrobe. Because as soon as you put your church clothes on and start out the door, the baby will throw up all over you. When you happen to be the pastor, having a backup outfit is not just a nice idea, it's critical. You don't want to stand in the pulpit with baby puke adorning your best silk blouse. And you can't make excuses to the congregation for being late because you had to go back and change clothes. I learned about Plan B the hard way, and I want to tell you: it was stressful.

Lord, Give Me Serenity

Some days I thought the stress would overwhelm me. How could I be a pastor, a counselor, a police chaplain, a wife, a mother, a daughter, a sister, an aunt, a friend? How could I do it all?

Many women in public life put on a front in times of great stress. Pastors are even more likely to do this because we're supposed to have it all together. But I didn't have it all together. Graduating from seminary made me the Reverend Dr. Suzan Johnson, but it didn't turn me into Superchristian. I don't have a cape. I can't fly like a speeding bullet or leap tall buildings in a single bound. I'm very human, just like you.

While I was learning to cope with the new blessing of motherhood, I latched on to a prayer that I had always loved but never fully comprehended. It's called the Serenity Prayer, written by Reinhold Niebuhr, and many times it sewed the threads of my soul back together when I was coming unraveled.

> God, give us grace to accept with serenity the things that cannot be changed, courage to change the things which should be changed, and the wisdom to distinguish the one from the other.[1]

Let me give you an example of how the Lord has answered this prayer for me. I have two sons now. Samuel David is five, and Christopher Daniel is almost three. One of the biggest adjustments I've had to make is learning how to write sermons with cartoons blaring in the background. My boys know that Mommy is a preacher and that I go to church all the time. But that's the extent of their concept of my role as a pastor. It doesn't matter if I'm in a very high spiritual moment with God, when that purple dinosaur comes on TV, they want Mommy to watch Barney with them. So I do because I understand that I won't ever have a second chance to go back and relive lost moments with two precious little boys.

God still gets some good sermons out of me, but I occasionally lose my peace of mind in the process. Then I have to allow his grace to give me the serenity to accept that my boys' need for my attention is something I can't change right now. All too soon they'll be grown up and won't need their mommy. Then I'll have to make another adjustment and learn how to write sermons without the jarring background noise, without sticky little hands pulling on my skirt, and without sweet little voices yelling, "Mom, Barney's on!"

Maybe that lesson won't be as hard to learn. Or maybe it will be even harder. But God's grace will help me accept it with serenity.

Stress Is a Distraction

The stresses of combining marriage, motherhood, and ministry drove me back into God's Word. As I spent time allowing Scripture to confront my innermost feelings, I came to understand that it is important not to become distracted from my true mission. Stress is a distraction that keeps me from fulfilling God's call on my life. I can't be all things to all people; I have to focus on being what God wants me to be and doing what he wants me to do.

You may not be in full-time ministry, but the same thing applies to you. Whatever you are called to do in life, you must learn how to keep stress from distracting you or destroying your peace of mind. You can learn to live with what Scripture describes as the peace that "surpasses all understanding" (Phil. 4:7).

Right now, are you so stressed that you can't be blessed? Do you wonder if you can ever change gears, put yourself in reverse, and turn that way of thinking around? You can. I'm not an expert. Not a doctor. Not a psychologist. Not a supersaint. I am a woman who has rediscovered some spiritual principles that helped me rearrange my priorities and change my thinking. In the process, I discovered I was too blessed to be stressed.

Things are always changing. People. Places. Situations. Circumstances. They flow in and out of our lives and sometimes turn our lives inside out. But one thing can be unchanging and constant in your life—God. He "is the same yesterday, today, and forever" (Heb. 13:8). And he has blessings prepared for you. Blessings that will transform you. Blessings that will keep you sane when the rest of the world goes crazy. Blessings that will give you a firm grip when life seems to be more than you can handle.

Perhaps you feel you are in a tough place where there are deep valleys, steep mountains, and winding, curving roads. The Bible says God will fill every valley, bring low every mountain, and make the crooked places straight and the rough ways smooth (Luke 3:5). God can help you straighten it all out.

God created you and cares for you. The psalmist said that God knows our "downsitting" and our "uprising" (Ps. 139:2 KJV). Today I pray for your uprising from wherever you have been sitting down on life, on yourself, or on others who are close to you. In fact, before I go any farther, I want to invite you to join me in this prayer:

> *Dear Lord, I need your peace today, the peace that surpasses all understanding.*
> *I have crooked places that need to be made straight and rough places that need to be smoothed. I'm facing mountains I can't climb and valleys I can't cross. I need help. I need you, Lord.*
> *Help me to recognize that your peace within me is the expression of mental, emotional, and spiritual balance in my life. I have not had that balance, Lord, and today I ask you for it.*
> *God, I turn to you as the great Stress Reliever, and I release into your hands all the worries and anxieties and struggles of life. I will*

*cast my burdens on you and allow myself to relax into perfect
peace, poise, patience, and power.*
    Breathe on me, breath of God. Fill me with life anew. Amen.

You can learn the same spiritual sensitivity skills that I have
used to alleviate a whole lot of pain and heartache. That's my
goal in writing this book: helping you to become stronger and
stay strong, to get on course and stay there. Much of what I've
written comes from the Too Blessed to Be Stressed workshops
I have taught across the country at women's conferences, con-
ventions, and churches.

These events are usually standing room only. The Bible says that
when you've done all you know to do, then just stand (Eph. 6:13).
I sometimes laugh and tell those in the back of the room, "If you
need help to keep you standing, you came to the right place."

What makes these workshops so effective is the ability to
interact with the participants. The women often ask for honest
"talk back," and I share as a girlfriend whose life in many ways
mirrors their own. I may serve on a presidential advisory board,
but I still have to arrange for child care, make doctors' appoint-
ments, pay bills, balance the checkbook—all the mundane chores
of life that have to be tackled.

This book will not allow me to interact personally with you.
Yet I have endeavored to write as if we were talking heart to
heart, sister to sister. Sometimes I'll share my experiences with
you, and sometimes I'll preach you a little sermon. Will you try
to say "Amen" every now and then as you turn the pages?

Count Your Blessings

When upon life's billows you are tempest tossed,
When you are discouraged, thinking all is lost,
Count your many blessings, name them one by one,
And it will surprise you what the Lord hath done.

Chorus:
Count your blessings, name them one by one;
Count your blessings, see what God hath done;
Count your blessings, name them one by one;
Count your many blessings, see what God hath done.

So, amid the conflict, whether great or small,
Do not be discouraged, God is over all;
Count your many blessings, angels will attend,
Help and comfort give you to your journey's end.

Reverend Johnson Oatman Jr., a Methodist lay preacher and businessman from New Jersey, wrote this hymn of encouragement in the late nineteenth century. It quickly became a gospel favorite at home and in Great Britain. During the great Welsh revival of those days, the congregation sang "Count Your Blessings" at every service.

Whether you sing this song or not, you should be praising and thanking God every day. It's hard to remain stressed out when you stop and count your blessings. You'll find you are too blessed to be stressed!

Can I Get a Witness?

Preaching is my passion. It charges my batteries to watch people open their lives to God while I'm speaking.

When I preach to my congregation or to other mostly black crowds, I get feedback during the sermon. My culture relishes freedom of expression, so members of the congregation vocally encourage their preacher and cheer me on. I love hearing it. If I make a really good point and don't hear enough response, I'll let the congregation know by saying, "Can I get a witness?" or "Hello, somebody!" That's their cue to "Amen" me, and they never fail in their job.

By faith I believe you're going to be encouraged and strengthened by what I have to share in this book. When I come to a point I want to be sure you don't miss, I may prompt my invisible congregation of readers to respond. That's your opportunity to say something like "Amen," or "That's right," or "Come on, now!" or "Preach, sister."

Don't be bashful. When it finally begins to sink in that you are too blessed to be stressed, you will feel such release that you'll want to shout or dance or sing. Go for it! If others get stressed out about it, that's their problem.

Are you ready to begin? Let's go straight to the most important lesson: knowing Whose you are.

CHAPTER TWO

Know Whose You Are

I have no way of knowing what nation my ancestors might have come from, but I imagine it was Ghana. That's the West African nation I have adopted as my second homeland. I have even taken an Ashanti name, Adzoa, which means "woman born on Monday."

I'm a city girl from the Bronx who spent a lot of time in the rural South. I'm at home in both places. But when I'm in Ghana, I feel at home in a way I can't explain. I'm enchanted by the unspoiled beauty of the land—the fertile fields, abundant with cacao and coffee trees, the surging rivers that roll and crash their way into the ocean. I'm captivated by the warmth of the people, their sunny dispositions, and their generosity of spirit. Ghana stirs something deep within me. The roots of my family tree must be planted there.

I rediscovered my spiritual roots in Ghana as well. My experiences there reminded me that I am a child of the King.

Have you ever seen kings and queens? The pageantry of a royal ceremony is unforgettable, dazzling in its grandeur and majesty. Vivid images of Ghanaian royalty are etched in my memory, and the lesson God taught me there remains in my spirit. I want to share that lesson with you. Will you unleash your imagination and come with me on a visit to see the king?

We will leave from Accra, the crowded capital city on the Atlantic oceanfront. The busy road, which quickly narrows as we leave the outskirts of the city, becomes a winding dirt path that seems to lead to nowhere. At first we pass a few people walking by the roadside, women balancing huge waterpots or baskets on their heads. We notice a handful of huts dotting the scrubland. Then there's nothing. No signs of human habitation. As the hot sun beats down, we follow the dusty path for several hours, unsure if we'll ever stumble across another human being.

Eventually we hear drums beating in the distance. Soon we hear voices singing melodies we've never heard, with words we can't understand, but the rhythm connects with our spirits. We follow the music until we reach the source, a small village where the people are preparing to honor their king. We have entered the Ashanti region. It's a world away from Buckingham Palace and much less opulent, but the fanfare is equally impressive.

Women young and old are spreading a feast. Men are beating drums, and the king's sons, the heirs of the kingdom, are dancing. You can tell which ones belong to the royal family. They're draped in the Kenté cloth reserved for royalty. The vibrant colors and bold patterns of the Kenté dip and sway with the dancers, making a kaleidoscope of sight and sound.

Over there is the king's wife. She is swathed in yards of the resplendent royal fabric, with a matching headdress. Not all of the women have their heads covered; if they do, it usually signifies they're married. Younger women, so fresh and full of life, pay tribute to the matriarchs of the tribe.

The villagers have heard we are coming and run to greet us. High shrieks of excitement fill the air. Our hearts are racing, too, as if we have finally come home, as if we have found the thing we were longing for but couldn't express.

The drumming, the singing, and the happy laughter are contagious. Soon our feet are moving with the beat; it's impossible to remain still in the midst of so much joy.

Suddenly the intensity of the drums increases, and the attention of the crowd turns in one direction. Look! It's the king. Do you see him?

As he enters amid a regal procession, the people begin bowing toward him. One by one the villagers bring their gifts before him and present the delicacies they have prepared. Each family has a native dance or song to perform for the king. He is delighted by their offerings. At sunset a fire is lit, and the celebration continues into the night. No one wants to leave the presence of the king.

We Are Royalty

I have witnessed such royal ceremonies several times, and each time I am awestruck. Part of it has to do with seeing dark-skinned royalty, beautiful browns. I may be impressed by the European aristocracy, but they're not my people. Ghanaian kings and queens look like me, and somehow that makes me feel whole and complete.

But it's much more than a matter of ethnic pride. I learned something about my Christian faith by being in the presence of African royalty.

Self-assurance and self-confidence are evident in the royal family. They know they are the heirs to the kingdom. Their position is assured. As Christian royalty, we are assured of our place within the kingdom of God. The Bible says that not only are we God's children, but we are "joint heirs" with Jesus Christ (Rom. 8:17).

Other passages in Scripture say that through Christ we have been made "kings and priests" to God (Rev. 1:5–6; 5:9–10). The apostle Peter called us "a royal priesthood":

> You are a chosen generation, a royal priesthood, a holy nation,
> His own special people, that you may proclaim the praises of
> Him who called you out of darkness into His marvelous light;
> who once were not a people but are now the people of God,
> who had not obtained mercy but now have obtained mercy.
> (1 Peter 2:9–10)

We are special people. *Hello, somebody!*

To show their privileged status, members of the royal family wear special clothing, the beautiful Kenté fabric reserved for their use alone. As Christians, we also wear royal garments. When we come to Christ, we cast off our "filthy rags" of self-righteousness (Isa. 64:6), and he clothes us in "garments of salvation" and covers us "with the robe of righteousness, / As a bridegroom decks himself with ornaments, / And as a bride adorns herself with her jewels" (Isa. 61:10). My husband and I love to get all decked out for a night on the town. But as much as we enjoy that, it cannot compare with the thrill of knowing that we wear royal robes as kings and priests of God.

That's another lesson I learned in Africa: the joy of being with the king. As I watched the Ghanaians dancing and singing before their king, their infectious joy and happy rhythms reminded me of a good old Baptist church service, at least the kind of Baptist church I grew up in and now pastor. When we start singing and praising King Jesus, it is impossible to sit still. There's too much joy to contain; some of it just has to come out—through our feet and our hands as well as our mouths.

It mystifies me how some Christians can come to church and sit in their pews like deadwood, sanctified and petrified. We should be bowing before our King in reverence. We should be dancing and singing for joy. We should bring an offering when we come into his presence. I'm not only talking about a financial offering, although worship includes giving. I'm also talking about offering ourselves as "a living sacrifice" to God, which is our "reasonable service" (Rom. 12:1). That is how to worship the King.

I will never forget lingering by the fire, under a starlit African sky, with people who were happy and warmed by the presence of their king. How much more should we desire to linger in the warmth of God's presence. In his presence are "fullness of joy" and "pleasures forevermore" (Ps. 16:11).

I have discovered Whose I am. I am a child of the King.

A Child of the King

My Father is rich in houses and lands,
He holdeth the wealth of the world in His hands!
Of rubies and diamonds, of silver and gold,
His coffers are full, He has riches untold.

Chorus:
I'm a child of the King, A child of the King:
With Jesus my Savior, I'm a child of the King!

I once was an outcast stranger on earth,
A sinner by choice, and an alien by birth,
But I've been adopted, my name's written down,
An heir to a mansion, a robe, and a crown.

Harriet Buell wrote this song while walking home from church on a Sunday morning in 1877. I can't help wondering what the pastor's sermon text was that day. Perhaps it was 1 John 3:1: "Behold what manner of love the Father has bestowed on us, that we should be called children of God!"

Remember this: you are a child of the King; you come from royal stock. You're a joint heir with Jesus Christ. You've inherited the riches of Christ, and you are seated with him in heavenly places. Daughter of God, lift up your head and sing!

All-the-Way Woman

I spoke at a Christian women's conference recently in Oakland, California. A unique father-son team, the Reverends J. Alfred Smith Sr. and Jr., are pastors of the Allen Temple Baptist Church there. How delightful it was to be in a church that affirmed women and celebrated their gifts. Many places have not welcomed us, and many pulpits have been closed to us. So it's always refreshing to be with brothers, like the Smiths, who have made a place for the sisters.

Some three hundred women gathered over that weekend to celebrate the sheer joy of being all-the-way women. There were older women, younger women, taller sisters, shorter sisters, thinner ones, plumper ones, some who were financially blessed, and some who were struggling to keep food on the table, but we were all God's women. And it felt good to proclaim our status, just as God created us, and to claim our blessings.

We not only claimed our blessings, however; we accepted our responsibilities. Women who understand Whose we are go all the way. We plan. We follow through. We complete the tasks before us. We make provisions for those in our care. All-the-way women carry the ball all the way to the finish line. We realize that God went all the way for us by giving Jesus Christ, his Son, so that we might have everlasting life.

All-the-way women do not make excuses for our gifts and callings. When God calls us to do something and equips us for the assignment, we get up and do it.

I make no apologies for being a woman. And I make no apologies for being a woman in ministry. If God didn't want me to be in the ministry, he would not have called me. If he didn't want me to preach, he would not have shut this fire up in my bones. If I couldn't preach, I believe I would spontaneously combust. I even preach in my dreams. That's one of the ways I knew God was calling me into the ministry in my early twenties; I would be sound asleep and wake up preaching.

I'm an all-the-way woman, and I'm going all the way with God. *Can I get a witness?*

Women Are Included

You are God's woman. Don't apologize, don't make excuses, and don't try to change what God has done in you and through you. There is a place for you in God's kingdom. You belong.

In a monarchy, there are both kings and queens. No earthly kingdom is complete without the queens. God's kingdom is the same. He has both sons and daughters. We are included.

I believe God enjoys diversity. He created men, and he created women. He made people different colors. I don't know why, but he did. Why did he make the sky blue, the grass green, the sun bright yellow, and the moon milky white? Perhaps God picked up his divine paintbrush at the dawn of creation and told the angels, "Let's put a little color, a little pizzazz, on this planet I've just made."

For whatever reason, human beings are diverse racially; we belong to different ethnic groups. And men and women are very different physically as well as emotionally. But when it comes to spiritual things, we are all the same. There is complete equality among God's children. Heaven doesn't need an affirmative action program. God's kingdom has always been inclusive.

That's news to some people. In many churches you seldom hear a sermon about women in the Bible. As a result, many Christians have never realized that women play a significant role in Scripture. But if you read the fine print, you'll discover we're all over the place. We're in the Old Testament, as judges and prophetesses. We're in the New Testament, as teachers and church leaders. There was even a group of women disciples who traveled with Jesus and helped him in his ministry (Luke 8:1–3; 23:49–55; 24:1–10, 22–24; Acts 1:13–14).

Paul wrote the church at Philippi and asked them to remember two women "who labored with me in the gospel" (Phil. 4:3).

In other words, he was saying, "Don't have selective memory when it comes to speaking about the sisters." Those women were colaborers, working side by side with Paul and Clement and the rest of the leaders of that church.

Some women become upset that the language of the Bible is not more inclusive, that it says only *he* or *him* when it applies to both men and women. But that's a reflection of the limitations of language in general. There are enough passages that specify both men and women to let us know that we're included. And many of the newer Bible translations give us a clearer understanding of that concept.

Scripture plainly says that *all* people are equal in God's sight. "There is neither Jew nor Greek [no racial divisions], there is neither slave nor free [no class divisions], there is neither male nor female [no gender divisions]; for you are all one in Christ Jesus" (Gal. 3:28).

When I read a verse in Scripture that addresses "the brothers," I know it includes "the sisters" as well. We are "one in Christ Jesus." If others think I'm *not* included because I'm a woman, or because I'm black, I'm not going to let them rain on my parade. I'm just going to keep doing what God has called me to do.

Hallelujah, I'm included! And so are you.

Women Leaders in the Early Church

I commend to you *Phoebe* our sister, who is a servant of the church in Cenchrea. . . .

Greet *Priscilla* and Aquila, my fellow workers in Christ Jesus. . . .

Greet *Mary*, who labored much for us.

Greet Andronicus and *Junia* . . . who are of note among the apostles. . . .

Greet *Tryphena* and *Tryphosa*, who have labored in the Lord. Greet the beloved *Persis*, who labored much in the Lord.

Greet Rufus, chosen in the Lord, and *his mother* and mine. . . .

Greet Philologus and *Julia*, Nereus and *his sister*, and Olympas. (Rom. 16:1–15 , italics added)

In his greetings in his epistle to the Romans, Paul calls twenty-nine people by name; ten of them were women. Some were church leaders. Phoebe was probably the one who delivered Paul's letter to Rome. Most Bible versions call Phoebe a "servant" or a "deaconess" of the church. But the Greek phrase used here literally means "a minister of the church."

We know from other passages that Priscilla was a gifted teacher. Four women, Mary, Tryphena, Tryphosa, and Persis, are called "laborers." The Greek phrase used to describe them means "a fellow worker in a common trade." It implies equality.

Junia was an apostle. In the Middle Ages, Bible translators began putting an *s* on the end of *Junia* to make it masculine; *Junias*, however, was an unknown name in Roman culture. Some scholars interpret this verse to mean that the apostles held Andronicus and Junia in high regard. But early church writings clearly identified them as apostles.

Women are included!

Don't Give Away Your Joy

By now you should be singing and shouting. You are God's woman. You are included. You are royalty. If that doesn't put the joy of God in your heart, then somebody needs to pronounce you DOA and note the time of death.

One of the songs my ancestors sang has carried over into our contemporary church tradition. I love to sing it.

> This joy that I have,
> the world didn't give it to me. . . .

> The world didn't give it,
> and the world can't take it away.
> This joy that I have,
> Jesus gave it to me. . . .
> Jesus gave it to me,
> and the world can't take it away.

When you gave your life to Jesus, Jesus gave new life to you. This new life in Christ was accompanied by a gift for you, a gift of the Holy Spirit and Jesus' joy. In fact, God's Word says that right now he is interceding for us in heaven, so that you and I will have joy (John 15–17).

You have joy. Jesus gave it to you. Don't let the world take it away. Don't let people or circumstances steal your joy. Difficult situations *will* come into your life; there is no way to escape them. "In the world you will have tribulation," Jesus said, "but be of good cheer, I have overcome the world" (John 16:33). When the trials of life come your way, you don't have to be defeated and depressed. Be of good cheer. Hold on to your joy.

If you've lost your joy, retrieve it. Tell yourself every day, "I am God's woman. Jesus gave me joy. I am a woman of joy." Take dominion over whatever tries to interfere with your joy. Remember Whose you are.

We Are Family

One thing that will help you keep your joy is to be part of a loving, caring, joyful church family. You have sisters and brothers. You're part of the family of God. And you can have a family reunion every Sunday.

I was born into a two-denomination, one-Lord household. My father was a Baptist from Virginia, and my mother was a Presbyterian from North Carolina. They met on her first day in the big city. My father had left home at age fifteen, after his parents died, and migrated to the North. He sent most of his paycheck back home to support his nieces and nephews, who had also lost their parents.

Dad became one of the first black trolley car drivers in New York City. He had a long, successful career with the Transit Authority. By the time he was forty, when he met my mother, he had already raised an entire family. In a sense, then, my brother and I were his second family. We grew up in a loving environment of extended family, and we enjoyed the nurturing of two church families as well.

My parents loved the Lord and they loved each other, but both really loved the church traditions they had been raised in. So they decided not to let which church their children would attend become an issue; we went to both churches.

Finding a Church Family

If you are without a church family and desire to be led to one that will meet your needs, here are some tips for you.

- Pray and ask God for a church family where you will be accepted, a body of believers you can accept as God's manifestation of love on earth.
- Allow the Holy Spirit to direct you. Ask friends for recommendations of churches that have appealed to them and ask why they liked them.
- Call or write a prospective church, and ask for a statement of faith. Find out what they believe, and ask what programs are available to meet your family's special needs (children's ministry, singles program, missions outreach, Christian education, Mothers' Day Out, etc.).
- Try to have an idea of how far you are willing to travel each week.
- Pick a church and visit. When you get home, discuss the worship experience with your family. Were the people friendly? Did they make you feel at home? Did you enjoy

the praise and worship music? Was God's presence evident in the service? Did the pastor preach a strong Bible message? (It doesn't matter how educated or articulate or charismatic the pastor is; what matters is that he or she preaches the Word.)

■ Pray again. Ask for God's confirmation if the church you have visited is where you are supposed to be.

■ When you choose a church, don't just drop in now and then for a visit. Attend regularly. Get involved. Make friends. Volunteer. Develop your spiritual gifts. You need a church where you will be ministered to, and you need a place where you can minister to others.

We lived on 144th Street in Harlem in my early childhood. On Sunday mornings my brother and I walked to 137th Street and attended Rendall Memorial Presbyterian with my mother. The Presbyterians did not have very long church services, so we were there for about an hour. By noon the three of us would be walking the eight blocks over to 145th Street to join my father at his church, Union Baptist. The Baptists were just getting warmed up by then, and we usually arrived during the last couple of songs before the sermon.

What an important lesson I learned in our two-denomination, one-Lord home! For my parents, it was not all that important which church we went to; what was important was that we understood that we were in the family of God. And the added blessing was that we had two very supportive and helpful church families to encourage us through all of our various stages of development.

I learned a biblical model of wholeness back in Harlem. Most of the families in our two churches had come from the South, and we were part of the rising black middle class in New York. There was tremendous unity among family and friends, and it was very similar to the way the Bible describes the first believers. We knew what it was to share and to have "all things in common" (Acts 2:44). We anticipated when there would be lack and when there would be plenty. No one ever had to ask; we knew when there was a need, and we did whatever we could to meet it. We took care of our brothers and sisters. We were family.

That is the kind of environment I want to provide for my children today. My husband belongs to the same denomination I do, but he was well established in his church by the time we met. So we're a two-church, one-Lord family. Most Sundays, Ron goes to his church. Sometimes our boys go with him, and sometimes they stay with me. We have two wonderful church families, a tremendous support system of love and nurture for us and our children.

You can have the same kind of fellowship and encouragement. It is never too late to join the family of God and to find a church family. To grow spiritually, you need to experience a healthy church environment. You must have a context that supports your claim to Christ on at least a weekly basis. If your identification with Christ is clear, then you need to be with others who are not having an identity crisis. You need to be with family.

Once you're in the family—when you know Whose you are—you will find the freedom to be who you are. And that's the next lesson: remember who you are.

CHAPTER THREE

Know Who You Are

"Suzan Denise Johnson, remember who you are!"

At sixteen I was already a head taller than my silver-haired grandmother, who had stretched to her full height of five feet to deliver her customary admonition.

"Yes, ma'am," I dutifully replied. I avoided the temptation to slam the door on my way out, but I defiantly held hands with my boyfriend.

Remember who you are, I silently fumed. *Why does she have to say that every time I leave the house?*

Earlier she had spotted us on the sofa, sitting entirely too close together in her judgment. She jumped all over poor Calvin, the object of my romantic interest that summer. "You don't know her well enough to be in her face like that. You two need to separate."

I was mortified. But I was determined to get her permission to go out with Calvin that evening, so I followed her into the kitchen.

31

Leona Fisher Starnes Thomas was not an easy woman to persuade. She was a petite dynamo with a mission in life: to keep me in line and make sure that my spitfire, which I had inherited from her, did not get out of control. Mama, as our family affectionately called her, was determined to make me a lady—a lady worthy of my southern heritage and my family name—and she pursued that goal with tenacity.

"I don't care what everybody else is doing," she said when I broached the subject of going out with Calvin. "You're not everybody else. And you're too young to be dating."

"I'm already in college, Mama."

"You may be in college, Miss Priss, but you're only sixteen."

I had blazed through prep school and was now tackling college. I thought I was grown up and knew everything. Mama thought otherwise. She did not want me to "blow my blessing" with some teenage boy whose hormones were running wild. She knew that one moment of passion could destroy all my dreams.

She reluctantly gave her permission: "I'm going to let you go out, but you better remember who you are." And later, when we left, she followed us to the door and repeated that refrain.

My grandmother issued an instruction to remember our heritage every single time my brother or I left the house, whether we were going on a date, or to a school event, or to a friend's house. "Remember who you are."

In other words, "You come from a good family line, a family that has spent a lifetime investing in you. And at all times, whether I am present or not, you should act accordingly." I may have flinched every time she said it, but her strategy worked. I never forget who I am.

I believe God tries to convey the same message to us every day. The Holy Spirit whispers to our hearts, *Remember who you are.*

You and I are from a holy and royal family line, and at all times, whether we can see or feel his presence, we are called to exhibit a "Christ in us" attitude. Whenever Satan entices you to "blow your blessing" for a moment of sin—whatever form the temptation might take—remember who you are.

Celebrating Who We Are

I think it's time we celebrated who we are as women, in general, and as women of God, in particular. We can celebrate both our similarities and our differences. We may not look alike, we may have different gifts and abilities, but we are connected in the Spirit. We share a common bond in Christ but speak with different voices and from different life experiences. Each of us has something unique to offer.

That's good. I don't want to be like everyone else. Some women like it simple, and others like it soft; some prefer life with a little spice, and some can take it with salsa. I happen to like mine with a little soul. *Vive la différence!*

The way we approach life varies according to our tastes, our culture, our environment—all the forces that shape us and make us who we are. But most of all, it depends on how we relate to God. When we appreciate Whose we are, we are able to respond favorably to others who are also in the Spirit, even if their approaches are not the same as our own. We can celebrate who we are.

I want to share with you some of the people and events that have shaped me as a woman, as a New Yorker with southern roots, as an African American, and as a Christian. All these influences have made me who I am. As you read about my background, think about the influences that have shaped your life and made you who you are. Your experiences may have been a world apart from mine, yet I believe you will discover some common threads in our lives.

One thing I know we both have experienced is the tremendous influence of the media, particularly television. What a contrast to even a few decades ago. Television was just coming into its own during the late 1950s when I was born. People were so excited about owning a television set that their entertainment centered on the little box in the living room.

Up until then, life was pretty much black-and-white. There was little color in life or on television. I can remember the entire family pulling our chairs up to the television set to watch the *Wizard of Oz*. The movie aired annually, and it was a big event. At the point in the movie where the tornado deposits Dorothy in the land of Oz, the film changes from black-and-white to color. The contrast is startling, and the Technicolor images of the make-believe land were dazzling, especially at a time when most television programs were still monochrome.

A Civil Rights Baby

The change from black-and-white to color in the *Wizard of Oz* could be a metaphor for life in the late fifties and early sixties. Our society was emerging from decades of enforced segregation, and people of color were entering the mainstream of American life. That's one of the most potent influences that shaped me as a woman: I am a civil rights baby. I was born the year the Little Rock Nine entered Central High School under police escort.

My parents and many other families had moved to the North in the hopes their children would not have to live through the poverty and racism they had known in the South. They had grown up in the Jim Crow era, when the races were completely separated. There were separate schools for black children. Blacks rode in the back of the bus and in separate railroad cars. Public buildings had separate rest rooms and water fountains marked COLORED; buildings without separate facilities were marked WHITES ONLY. Most restaurants and hotels in the South refused to serve blacks; even well-known entertainers like Harry Belafonte were turned away.

When Martin Luther King Jr. organized the first march on Washington, in August 1963, my parents and all their friends rented buses and made the trip down to the nation's capital. They were eyewitnesses to that historic moment when Dr. King's powerful voice rang out with his masterpiece, the unforgettable "I Have a Dream."

I was too young to attend the march, but I remember watching it on television. I also remember going to the Freedom Schools held on Saturdays in the churches of our community. Parents organized the classes so that their children could learn what it would take for black people to be free. I can still sing the old freedom songs, and I remember the tremendous joy attached to those sessions. Under the leadership of Dr. King and men like Wyatt Walker, Jesse Jackson, Andrew Young, and Adam Clayton Powell, momentum was building. Everybody was excited about civil rights—the end of Jim Crow was within our grasp.

When I was eight, my mother took me to Hunter College to see Martin Luther King. I was thrilled when we went backstage and got his autograph. It was the first and last time I would get to see him in person. Three years later, we were on the way to the shopping mall when the car radio delivered the awful news: our hero had been felled. Mother turned the car around and headed straight home. We passed people sobbing in the streets as they heard the news of the assassination. The loss was incalculable, the pain inconsolable.

Those early experiences in the civil rights movement shaped me as a woman and as a pastor. Freedom School planted seeds in our spirits. It taught my generation that we could soar, that we would not be bound by the things that had limited our predecessors. We learned to be proud of who we were, and our role models were people who were not afraid to die for the cause of freedom.

As a result of my exposure to the marches, boycotts, and nonviolent demonstrations against injustice and racism, I have always been drawn to justice issues. I observed firsthand how the black churches formed the very foundation of the civil rights movement. So I use that model in my ministry, fighting the freedom issues of today from my pulpit.

A Southern Lady

In addition to being born into a civil rights consciousness, I was born into a close-knit family whose roots were firmly planted in the South. My grandmother succeeded in her mission of turning me into a southern lady, with all that connotes. But it was quite a challenge, and it was a collective effort.

In the early sixties, many black families sent their children to the South during the summers. My brother, Ronald, and I loved the annual ritual. But the purpose of those trips was more than a celebration of our childhood years. My southern relatives were also charged with helping to carefully guide our rites of passage into adulthood.

New York schools always closed on the last weekday in June. The very next morning Ronald and I would board a Trailways bus headed for Concord, North Carolina, about thirty miles from Charlotte. I wasn't aware of it then, but in spite of the strides made in the civil rights movement, Jim Crow was still alive and well in the South. Because we were black, we could not fly, and there were certain places we could not stop. Trailways, which stopped locally in all the southern towns, was our safety route.

Securely tucked under my brother's arm as we got on the bus was a large shoe box. My mother had filled it with fried chicken, pound cake, ham sandwiches with mayonnaise, and sodas that had been frozen overnight and wrapped in tin foil. By the time we reached Washington, we would have eaten the fried chicken, and somewhere between there and North Carolina, which was another eight hours away, we would dig out the ham sandwiches. By then the sodas would be the right consistency to drink. To this day I prefer my ham sandwiches cold and soggy, just the way they came out of that shoe box on our bus trips.

Our lifestyle in New York was vastly different from that of the rural South. But one thing was the same: the focus on faith and family. Sunday was the most important day of the week. And at my grandmother's house, we observed it as the Sabbath. She did not allow wild playing or hard work such as cooking or ironing, so we spent all day Saturday in preparation for our day of rest. It took a *lot* of preparation to get me ready. I was the tomboy of all tomboys and never thought of wearing a dress or curling my hair unless someone made me. Mama made me. In fact, she made me wear a hat, little white gloves, stockings, and patent leather shoes to church.

We often drove to Monroe, another small town about thirty miles from Concord, to attend church with a number of our relatives. Our family members were deacons, ushers, and trustees at Blacks' Memorial Presbyterian. After church we began the visitation ritual. Lunch would be a feast, even though many of my relatives were very poor. We ate few vegetables at home in New York, but around Aunt Bess's table we enjoyed delicious home-grown tomatoes, string beans, okra, and creamed corn. At the dinner table everyone reminisced and swapped stories, and of course, we had to provide details on what our parents were doing and promise to deliver messages when we returned.

From Aunt Bess we went to visit Aunt Miss, who was blind. Aunt Miss dipped snuff, as many folks in those parts did. She would say, "Baby, come over here and kiss your Aunt Miss." I did, even though it was traumatic when I was younger. Southern hospitality required that she, too, have a dessert or delicacy to share with us. So we ate again.

Next we visited Aunt Edna, whose specialties were pound cakes and three-layer coconut cakes. Throughout my college days, Aunt Edna would bake pound cakes for me. She would send them with someone who was coming that way or ship them by Trailways. I always appreciated her generosity and her expression of love.

With all those visits, my grandmother was teaching us a lesson. She wanted us to remember that no matter how successful we were, these people were still our family. We were connected to them, and their love and support were things that money could not buy. It was another way of saying, "Remember who you are."

At my grandmother's house, everything we did turned into a learning experience. She was a gifted teacher whose lesson book was life itself. One day she was teaching me how to make biscuits. I stood at the kitchen counter, watching her small hands deftly roll and pat and shape the dough. Then she turned a Mason jar upside down and quickly cut out a dozen or so perfectly round biscuits. As she picked up the rolling pin to prepare another panful, she said, "Be careful how you roll things, Suzan. Don't let anybody talk you into rolling one of those joints." Who else would have thought to equate rolling out biscuit dough with the evils of smoking marijuana?

My grandmother also taught me courage and confidence. I attended a prestigious prep school in New York City, Riverdale Country School, where I was one of only two black students in the seventh grade. It was the height of the Black Power movement, and like most of my friends, I sported an Afro, a natural hairdo. One day a white classmate stuck her fingers in my hair and called it Brillo. I was humiliated.

When I told my grandmother about it the following summer, she said, "You go back there and hold your head up high. Don't change your hair, and don't you ever be ashamed of who you are. You paint that school black." She definitely was not talking about spray painting the walls of the school. It was her way of saying, "Don't be ashamed of being black. It's who you are. Don't compromise. Don't let anyone steal your identity."

I learned that lesson so well that in the ninth grade I was elected to the Student Council—the first black ever elected in my overwhelmingly white school. I had become confident and comfortable with who I was. So I did what my grandmother taught me. I painted that school black.

Who Are Your She-roes?

Women are usually the keepers of the culture, the ones who keep the family spirit alive. My grandmother and her sisters, my great-aunts, made sure we understood who we were. As children we loved hearing stories about the heroes and she-roes of their day, the men and women who made tremendous strides against the odds, those whose faith and courage were tested and proved.

Even now that I am an adult, revisiting these stories brings to life those celebratory moments from the past. These stories of my family's heritage and faith strengthen my understanding of who I am.

Who are some of your heroes and she-roes? Preserve your family's faith and culture by remembering and sharing their stories.

- Take a few moments to jot down some of the memorable stories about your family or church family. Have you shared these stories with your children? Is there a friend who is going through some rough spots who might be encouraged by the testimony of one of your she-roes? File these stories away in your memory, and share them when it's appropriate and helpful.
- If some of the older family members or friends with whom you shared some special moments are still alive, take a moment and drop them a line. A card that lets them know you are thinking of them will be a blessed moment in their day and yours.

A Christian Woman and Minister

I acquired my self-confidence as a woman and as an African American from my parents and my extended family. But another influence shaped my life, and it's perhaps the most important influence: the same people modeled Christ for me. I saw Christian principles in action every day of my life, and it made me who I am today.

Whether I was in the city, with our two wonderful church families there, or in the country churches with my southern relatives, faith was the cornerstone of my life. And that's probably why I ended up working in God's house, because I loved being there as a child.

Another one of my aunts, Annabelle Fisher Springs, ran a mission, a one-room schoolhouse up the block from my grandmother. She was not an ordained minister, but she was called to be a missionary. Aunt Pet, as she was known, gathered all the children in the community together and taught them about Jesus. In the summers, she held a vacation Bible school. We played rambunctiously in the hot sun for a while, then came inside and cooled off while Aunt Pet discipled us for several hours. I started taking piano lessons when I was four, so she enlisted me to play a song every day. At a big pageant at the end of summer, we crowned a king and a queen. But we learned that all of us were winners. We began to understand that Jesus made us victors.

At the house of yet another aunt, whom we called Bee, I first considered the possibility of women in ministry. She was one of my favorite aunts, my mother's sister, and worked as assistant to the president of Barber Scotia, a black Presbyterian college in Concord. The students loved to come to Miss P's (her last name was Porcher) on the weekends. Many of the students were too far away or too poor to go home for a visit during the school year, so my aunt opened her home to them.

One of the students, a senior at Scotia, was named Katie Cannon. She loved Miss P and visited frequently. Katie always talked about wanting to go into the ministry, and in those days I had never heard of a woman wanting to preach or going to seminary. Most people thought the idea was far-fetched. But Katie Cannon was a trailblazer. She became the first black woman to earn a doctorate from Union Theological Seminary, and the first black woman ordained in the Presbyterian church. I followed in her footsteps a few years later when I entered seminary and then became a trailblazer in my own denomination.

As the first female minister I ever met, Katie Cannon had a tremendous influence on me. So did all the men and women, pastors and parishioners alike, who taught me to love God, to love being in God's house, and to love being who God made me. They helped me discover who I am.

Are You Shaping Other Women?

Who were the formative influences in your life, the people who helped you discover who you are? One of the most exciting things you can do is to pass that blessing along, to help shape others as Christian women.

I may have forgotten some of their names over the years, but I have never forgotten the influence of those in my church family. And the informal interaction as much as the structured teaching molded our lives. Older members of our congregation would speak to the younger ones about our goals. They didn't just encourage kids to stay in school. They would say, "Where are you going to college?" Or, "Do you have a job lined up for the summer?" They expected us to excel, and they helped us achieve our dreams. And we did.

That is why it is so important for you not only to be in the household of faith but also to share with others your gifts and knowledge. Younger women need you. Older women need you. And you need them. You have talents and skills that can benefit them. It doesn't take a lot of education or experience to influence others. It just takes a willingness to offer encouragement and direction. Share your love and knowledge of God with others.

When you know who you are, you can help others discover who they are.

Celebrating Faith and Culture

Growing up, I found it impossible to separate church and family and heritage. Our culture was tied into our faith, not separated from it. It's who we were.

Always lift up who you are as you come closer to your understanding of Whose you are. I am a woman. I am a Christian. I am also an African American. I am a northerner with southern roots. These are not deficits; they are distinctions. They are all blessings.

Look for ways to blend your beliefs with your blessings.

Members of my congregation do this by dressing in African attire several Sundays each year. It strengthens our understanding of our heritage and our appreciation of who we are. There is no power in the distinctive, colorful clothes we wear; the power lies in making the connection that God made us who we are. "Red and yellow, black and white, we are precious in his sight." Jesus loves and celebrates our diversity; so should we.

People anticipate with enthusiasm the days we honor our heritage. Several have enjoyed it so much that they adopted African dress as their weekly attire; they are proud of who they are.

Be intentional about enjoying your culture while learning to respect the great diversity within our nation and within the body of Christ.

Don't Forget Who You Are

Once you learn who you are, don't forget it. Don't get too big for your britches. Don't forget those who invested their time and treasure in you, those who made sacrifices to help you get where you are in life.

"Remember who you are." *Hello, somebody*!

Toward the end of the year I spent as a White House fellow, we were invited to the Oval Office for a photo session for the fellowship program's thirtieth anniversary commemorative book. President Clinton asked me to pray with him that day, so I did. I don't know how I managed to get the words out. The Lord had to help me because all I could think about was that here I was, a Baptist preacher who got her start in life in a walk-up tenement on 144th Street in Harlem, and now I was in the White House, praying with the president of the United States.

A Prayer of Susanna Wesley

I have found, O God, that my peace and happiness depend much on my own opinion of myself and not on that of others. It is the inward sentiments I have of myself that raise or deject me. . . . Help me not to contend with men's interests, prejudices, and passions, that rarely admit of a calm dispute, when it can be innocently avoided. May I be so far a lover of myself as to prefer the peace and tranquility of my own mind before that of others, and if, after doing all that I can to make others happy, they yet remain obstinately bent to follow those ways that lead to misery, I leave them to Thy mercy. Amen.[1]

Women have always struggled to define themselves in male-dominated societies. In the early 1700s one woman who learned to be confident of her identity was the mother of the famous Wesleys of England. At age nineteen, Susanna Annesley, the twenty-fifth (and last!) child of a famous Nonconformist pastor, married Samuel Wesley, an Anglican minister. In addition to being a pastor's wife and managing a busy household, Susanna home schooled her children, even writing some of their textbooks, and studied theology and church history.

When her husband was away on church business, she entered the pulpit and read his sermons to the congregation. Her doing that raised a few eyebrows, but no one could dispute that Susanna was the most qualified person in the parish. Her fifteenth child, John, and her seventeenth, Charles, followed their father—and mother—into the ministry, becoming the founders of the Methodist church.

How did Susanna Wesley cope with the pressures of life? John Wesley wrote in his journal that his mother never let anything interfere with her quiet time with God. Many women think they're too busy to pray; Susanna Wesley knew she was too busy *not* to pray. And it's obvious from this brief prayer that she had spent enough time with God to know who she was as well as Whose she was.

I'll also never forget the day I got my official credentials that allowed me access to the White House. Going through the placement process had been a whirlwind of activity—interviews, paperwork, screenings for security clearance. Until a permanent pass was issued, I had to check in with the guards at the gate just to get on the grounds and get to my office. Then I received my White House credentials.

That first day I sailed through the gates and nobody stopped me, I was standing on the front lawn of the White House when it suddenly hit me: *I belong here.* I had to stop and look around for a minute as it sank in that it was all right for me to be freely roaming around one of the world's most famous buildings, the symbol of everything my country stands for. I couldn't contain myself. I just threw my hands in the air and said, "Thank you, Lord!"

That was what my mother and father scrimped and saved and sacrificed for. That was why all those relatives in Concord and Monroe were telling me to "keep the faith" and keep going forward. I stood there on the White House lawn for all of my family. I stood there for all those freedom-seeking African Americans who taught me I could soar, the men and women who told me to be proud and stand tall. Their legacy to me was all wrapped up in my going through the front door of the White House. I had gone from the outhouse—some of the relatives I stayed with in the South did not have plumbing until the 1980s—to the White House.

Praise God, that's who I am.

CHAPTER FOUR

Know Where You're Going

I pushed open the heavy door marked DEAN OF STUDENTS. The occupant of the office, Shelton Forrest, was the last reference I needed to complete my application for law school.

"Come in, please, Sujay." He drew the name out in melliflu-ous tones that held a hint of Jamaica. "So tell me about this plan of yours to study law. I was surprised to hear about it."

Everybody was surprised about it. Even me. The idea had been hatched out of desperation. I was nineteen and about to finish a fine arts degree at Emerson College in Boston. My pas-sion was performing. But I never could have asked my family to pay for a college education just so I could be an entertainer or an actress. I had to pick a field they would support, and a major in mass communications was the closest thing to per-forming that would still be considered legitimate in their eyes.

I was about to graduate and, like most fine arts students, didn't have a job lined up. I was academically smart, but still too young to know where I was going in life. And when you come from a conservative, traditional family like mine, you feel a compelling need to have "a bird in the hand." The bird I had picked was a law degree. My brother was an assistant district attorney, doing very well and garnering the accolades of the family. So I tried to pour myself into that mold. I took the LSATs, the law school entrance exams. I hated the exams, and my feelings showed in my scores. But I went ahead and started gathering references from college professors to bolster my law school application. That was what led me to Dean Forrest's office. He was the last on my list.

"You know I'll be happy to write a reference for you." He paused a beat, stroking the beard that sheltered his face, which was the color of rich chocolate mocha. "But first I want you to tell me why you decided on law school."

"I want to go into entertainment law," I said.

"And what does an entertainment lawyer do?" He knew I despised details and did not enjoy reading very much—qualifications any lawyer needed, especially an entertainment lawyer involved in complicated contract negotiations.

"I don't know that much about it," I admitted. Actually I didn't have a clue. Entertainment law sounded like something that would be a bridge with the performing world and still earn the respect of my family.

Shelton Forrest was my mentor. When my father had died the previous semester, he had counseled me and helped me get through the loss. He knew me well, knew that I was a bird who needed to fly. And it was his job to push me out of the nest.

"Sujay," he said, "you have acted in, directed, or helped produce every theater performance on this campus. You come alive when you're on stage. You're a talented composer and performer. Do you not trust yourself enough to get a job in that field?"

"Well, yes. But my family expects me to do something more respectable, more—I don't know—more stable and secure, I guess."

"You believe in God, don't you? You're always at St. Paul's, singing in the choir or working in one of their productions. Did you ever consider that God gave you these talents, this desire to be in the limelight?" Perhaps he was sensing the gifts and calling of God on my life even then. "What is it that you really want to do?" he asked.

"I want to be in television." That was what I loved. That was where my heart was. "I want to produce. I want to be on the air. I want to do it all."

"Then that's what you need to do. I could write a reference for law school for you, but that's really not what is right for you."

He was correct. I was not cut out for law school. Relieved that a trusted advisor had recognized that, I summoned my courage and abandoned my ill-conceived plan.

Instead of applying to law school, I applied with several placement services and found a program called Career Opportunities (COP). They set up a telephone interview with the station manager and producer of WLJA-TV in Washington, D.C., who hired me sight unseen as a floor producer for a local political show. My television career was launched.

Determine Your Destination

At nineteen I was determined and ambitious, but I didn't know where I was going in life. And when you don't know where you're going, how will you know when you get there?

I travel almost weekly. When I arrive at the airport, I cannot just jump on any plane. I have to know in advance which flight I'm taking and the gate from which it will depart. And the plane cannot take off without a flight plan to reach its destination.

Just as a plane or a ship must chart a course before the journey, so must we. Having a clear idea of where we are heading will eliminate, or at least reduce, the amount of stress in our lives. We don't always end up exactly where we are aiming; life offers no guarantees. But we can stay on a designated course until God guides us in a different direction. You may have to take a detour, but don't get derailed—stay on track.

Like a river, life has a certain flow. Those who know where they're going learn to plunge into the waters. Sometimes the water is rough, and sometimes there is a danger of running aground or diving into shallow water. But more often than not, life's waters are quite deep.

To make any journey, whether by sea or land or air, you need a guidance system—a map or chart, radar or sonar. Those of us in Jesus Christ have access to a divine guidance system. He will be our Pilot, our Navigator through life's journey.

Jesus, Savior, Pilot Me

Jesus, Savior, pilot me
Over life's tempestuous sea:
Unknown waves before me roll,
Hiding rocks and treach'rous shoal;
Chart and compass come from Thee—
Jesus, Savior, pilot me!

As a mother stills her child,
Thou canst hush the ocean wild;
Boist'rous waves obey Thy will
When Thou say'st to them, "Be still!"
Wondrous Sov'reign of the sea,
Jesus, Savior, pilot me!

A Presbyterian minister named Edward Hopper wrote this hymn, first published in 1871. Hopper pastored a small church in New York City, a missions outreach to the many seamen who sailed in and out of the harbor. The hymn became instantly popular with seafaring men who regularly relied on "chart and compass" for navigation.

As we navigate life's stormy seas, we can depend on Jesus to pilot us. He is our divine Chart and Compass. And how we need him! Even when we know where we're going, the going can be rough. If you find that life is not exactly smooth sailing, relax. You know the Pilot.

But the vehicle, the vessel, must have some partnership with the Guide. We must seek God's will when we begin to choose our direction and chart our course:

> Trust in the Lord with all your heart,
> And lean not on your own understanding;
> In all your ways acknowledge Him,
> And He shall direct your paths. (Prov. 3:5–6)

Following God-inspired and God-directed paths is what life is all about.

From experience I can say that having a clear idea of my destination in life has come from spending quality time with God. Certainly there are daily divine surprises, which surpass even my own understanding. That is because I cannot see the total picture; I cannot see exactly what God sees for me. But I try to follow the light he shines on my path.

Don't Lose Sight of the Light

The psalmist declared, "Your word," O Lord, "is a lamp to my feet / And a light to my path" (Ps. 119:105). When we keep the light of God's Word before us, we will not lose our way.

When I was twelve years old, I went on my first overnight sleep-out in the woods. It was at Camp Incarnation, an Episcopalian summer camp in Connecticut, where we enjoyed many outdoor activities, such as hiking and canoeing, that were unavailable in the city. To build self-confidence and foster a sense of independence, the older kids, those twelve to fourteen, were allowed to camp out overnight.

It was a big event for city kids to spend the night out under the stars. We were excited and eager to explore without the constant supervision of adult eyes. But first the counselors helped us find a campground and set up our tents. They set boundaries for us, giving us general guidelines where we could go. Then, before allowing us to freely roam the grounds, they hung a large lantern to mark the campsite. "If you wander away," they said, "look for the light. As long as you can see the light, you can make your way back."

That is sound advice for us as Christians: always look for the light. God, too, invites us to explore, but there is a light—the light of his Word—that remains constant for our gaze. Staying focused on the light is sometimes difficult, but it is vital for maintaining our sense of direction.

A church member recently called to inquire about a guest minister she had admired. "Pastor, you know the preacher who came one day to preach for us?" she said.

Since that didn't give me much to go on, I replied, "Well, we've had a lot of guests, and we have four services weekly. Perhaps you can narrow it down to a month or day of the week."

Then she realized that she hadn't given me enough information. I needed a much stronger clue to be able to focus on giving her an answer.

Many of us go through life blessed but unfocused. We know somewhere deep down inside what we want to say or do, but we don't always get it across. Multitalented people especially find it difficult to be clear on exactly what they want to do or where they're going. They jump around from school to school, church to church, project to project. They are everywhere and nowhere at the same time.

Some people can't put a résumé together or get through a job interview because they can't stay focused. You can't go into an interview and just say, "I need a job." You go in and tell the prospective employer what you bring to the position and how you can make a difference for that company.

I have interviewed many seminarians who wanted to work for my church. Many of them came in with the wrong intent; they were focused on a corporate model. They asked about salary and benefits and the number of days off. Some couldn't even answer the question about why they were in seminary. If I never heard an expression of love for God's people, then I knew they had no understanding of what it takes to be in pastoral ministry.

On the other hand, some seminarians came in with a humble attitude, demonstrating a servant's heart. You will create a position for that kind of person because he or she is focused on being a shepherd over God's flock.

All of God's people, not just seminarians, should be focused on doing something special, something specific. The Gospel of Luke says, "To whom much is given, from him much will be required" (12:48). We should not wander aimlessly through life, hoping that some purpose catches up with us. We must aim for something specific, even if we miss the target. So what if you miss the bull's-eye, as long as you get onto the canvas?

Too many Christians are wandering, not walking. They have never allowed God to set them on a path.

Charting Your Course

If you are not sure where you're going in life, now is the time to determine your destination and chart your course. In this chapter you will find an exercise called "Charting Your Course." If you are at a crossroads, I invite you to take a few minutes and work through this exercise. It will help you focus on your God-given desires and make a plan for moving forward.

As you make a list of your dreams and ideals, you will see that not every desire of your heart is something you are willing to put time into at this point in your life. For example, I loved performing in my college years; acting was my forte, although I did some singing and dancing. But for me to place professional acting as a goal right now would not be something I would have time to do. Nor have I laid any groundwork for success in that field. I haven't paid my dues, while others have committed years of their lives to professional training and gaining recognition in that field.

One of my college friends, Clifton Powell, is now appearing on quite a few shows on the major networks. I recently interviewed Clifton on a radio talk show. He had a ten-year plan for his acting career when he left college, and he stuck with it. In fact, Clifton exceeded the goals he originally set for himself. But he was willing to be a starving actor if that's what it took. I had had a taste of the good life after college and was not willing to go to that extreme. Therefore, acting may be a love of mine, but it is not a goal for me. I would have to scratch it off my list as I looked at it realistically.

Charting Your Course

Here is an exercise I frequently use with people who come into my office at transition times, when they are in the process of making a decision whether to go or stay or change directions.

Draw three columns on a piece of paper.
- Title the first column *Who Am I?* List all the roles in which you see yourself, with whatever titles you attribute to yourself: wife of (*name*), mother of (*name*), daughter of (*name*), sister of (*name*), best friend of (*name*), pastor, teacher, doctor, caregiver, gardener, golfer.
- Title the second column *Where Do I Want to Be?* In this column write down the things you have given serious thought to doing. Be realistic—are these things achievable?—but don't limit yourself. You might list such things as stand-up comedian, airline pilot, public speaker, restaurant owner, teacher.

■ Title the third column *What Will It Take to Get There?* Will going in this new direction require additional education, financial resources, new skills, new friends? What will it take? Write it down.

This exercise allows you to see your plans (or lack of plans) for your life, and to see if they are realistic and attainable. It will help you see if you're ready to pay the dues, to make the commitment necessary to reach your goals.

It will also help you prioritize your life and focus on the issues that are important for the present, setting aside for the moment secondary issues.

You may find that by redirecting your path, you can leave behind things that bring you stress, such as working at a job you really don't care for and aren't gifted for, or a person who constantly puts you down or holds you back.

Choose to chart your course for the blessed life, not the stressed life.

When I worked through this exercise recently, one of the things I put down under *Who Am I?* was that I am an aunt to Jessica and Charles, my only niece and nephew. As I wrote that down, something happened to me. I began to think how special these kids were to me. I had spent a significant amount of time with them when they were younger. In fact, I helped raise them. Yet now, as they were going to college and starting their professional careers, I barely knew them. It dawned on me that I was missing important moments in their lives.

It also reminded me of the wonderful times I had enjoyed with my aunts, and I hoped that I could recapture some of that same spirit by passing such a blessing on to them. But I had not spent a lot of time with Jessica and Charles lately, as my aunts had done with me.

Family is fundamental to me, so after working through this exercise, I made some decisions about what things I would focus on for the upcoming months. I chose to cut back in other areas of my life that were not as meaningful to me in order to put some time into my relationship with my niece and nephew.

Earlier I had made some changes that would enable me to spend more time with my husband and two young sons. Launching a new church in my neighborhood, which I will tell you more about shortly, cut out more than two hours of daily commuting and gave me more time at home. Also, I cut back on travel time by limiting most of my speaking engagements to the East Coast, which allows me to be back at home with my family each night.

Having a clear idea of where you're going, and what it will take to get there, will help you know where to channel your energy. Then the projects you choose to take on will be even more blessed because you will have the time and vitality needed to complete them successfully.

I find it such a tragedy to hear people nearing the end of their lives say things like, "If only I had done . . ." or "I wish I had had a chance to . . ." Don't wait until life's journey is nearly over before you decide where you're going. Make choices you can live with now. Determine your destination and chart your course. Make plans and goals. But be flexible enough to respond to God if he sends you in a different direction. When God is steering your course, he will clearly signal when a change in direction is coming.

A Change in My Direction

As I graduated from Emerson College, my mentor, Shelton Forrest, helped me chart my course for a career in television. But even then he had noticed a spark in me that signaled a higher calling.

I enjoyed my career in television and have never regretted following that path. But God gradually made clear to me that he was placing a different call on my life, a call into the Christian ministry. And once again, God positioned the right people in my path to direct me.

No matter where I was during my years in the television industry, a powerful magnet kept pulling at my soul: seminary. Those freewheeling discussions with Scotia students, especially Katie Cannon, had stirred a desire in me and challenged my way of thinking about ministry. Finally I started taking seminary courses at night. I had no clear ministry goals in mind; I just knew I wanted to be in seminary. I've always been a multifaceted person who likes to do more than one thing at a time. So I continued to juggle television and seminary as long as possible.

Eventually the competing time demands grew unmanageable. For example, my station was covering a hostage crisis in the District of Columbia. Things got intense just before the hostages were released, and one day we worked twenty straight hours; we couldn't leave the station because we didn't know the precise moment when the hostages would be released, and we had to be on the air to cover the story. There was no way I could keep up with that kind of time commitment and stay in seminary.

But it was not until the day God rear-ended me that I owned up to the fact that I had a very important decision to make. I had never had an automobile accident before that particular day. Within a twenty-four-hour period, however, three cars hit me. The third collision happened when a ball rolled out in front of my car. I knew a child would be close behind that ball, so I braked hard. A truck slammed into me from behind, crumpling my car.

Police arrived on the scene almost immediately, and they were concerned that I was injured or dazed by the accident. An officer said, "Is there someone we can call to stay with you? Do know anybody in this neighborhood?"

I looked around to get my bearings and was utterly amazed. I was squarely in front of my father's old church, Union Baptist. "You could see if my pastor is in there," I said, pointing across the street to the church. It was a weekday, at an hour when the pastor was usually not in. But God had arranged for him to be where I needed him, at the exact moment I needed him.

Reverend Ollie Wells ran out to the car. "Jay, are you okay?" he asked.

"I think so," I said, but the quaver in my voice indicated just how shaken I really was. I began telling him about my string of accidents. "Pastor, when is all this going to stop happening to me?"

"When you stop running from the call to preach," he answered gently.

About three years earlier I had shared with him that I felt God was calling me into the ministry. At that time, I could scarcely sleep at night. When I did doze off, I would be preaching in my dreams. Pastor Wells had perceived that God was changing my course before I did.

Now, worried that I might have internal injuries even though I appeared all right outwardly, the police called an ambulance. As I lay in the hospital emergency room, I clearly sensed God asking me, *Are you ready? Will you preach the gospel?*

When God has you laid out on a stretcher in the ER, he has your full attention. I said yes to God. And I've never had another car accident since that day.

All the Way My Savior Leads Me

All the way my Savior leads me;
What have I to ask beside?
Can I doubt His tender mercy,
Who thro' life has been my guide?
Heavenly peace, divinest comfort,
Here by faith in Him to dwell!
For I know whate'er befall me,
Jesus doeth all things well;

For I know whate'er befall me,
Jesus doeth all things well.

One morning in 1874 Fanny Crosby had a problem. Her rent was due, and she had no money. So she took her need to the Lord in prayer. Before long a visitor appeared at her door. There was certainly nothing unusual in that; the popular poet and hymn writer entertained many visitors. But as the man left, he pressed a bill into her hand. It was the exact amount she needed for the rent. With her need met, Fanny sat down and composed this hymn of thanksgiving to the Guide of her life.

Choosing God's Path

Even though I had affirmed my commitment to preach, I still tried to stay in the television industry while I finished seminary. Part of the reason was financial. How would I support myself? There were a few ordained women in ministry by then, but actual paying positions were almost nonexistent. I was hanging on to my steady salary while pursuing the ordained ministry until God got my attention again.

I had landed a job at Bronx Lebanon Hospital, working as the public relations director and frequently appearing on-camera in that capacity. I was also taking courses at Union Theological Seminary. All of Union's classes were offered during daytime hours, so it really required a full-time commitment. I was trying to get from the Bronx to Manhattan, take a class during my lunch break, and then get back to work. It was simply not possible.

On the day of my final exam in preaching, under Dr. James Forbes, I learned I would have to make an on-camera appearance for the hospital. A man whose family was still living in the Dominican Republic had made a dying wish to be reunited with them. The hospital had gone to great expense and effort to bring his family to New York, and I was supposed to handle the press conference.

I hated to do it, but I left my exam early and tried to make it across town to the hospital. But I got stuck in traffic on the 155th Street bridge, which connects Harlem to the Bronx. Now both projects would be unfinished. And it dawned on me that *unfinished* was an accurate picture of my life.

Sitting there in my car, with traffic virtually at a standstill, I seemed to hear God's voice: *You have to make a choice. You can't continue running back and forth. It's time to make a decision.* I not only reaffirmed my commitment to preach but also told God I would do it now. I would quit television completely and go into full-time ministry. And the moment I reached that decision, traffic opened up.

As soon as possible, I got to a phone and called the hospital. "Someone else will have to go on the air," I said. "I can't get there. I'll explain tomorrow."

I raced back to Union and finished my exam. The next morning I told the hospital that I had to resign because I was called to preach.

"You're going to do *what*?" people asked in disbelief. I reiterated my intention to enter full-time ministry. They were surprised because it seemed out of character. I was not the kind to stand by a patient's hospital bed and witness. I wasn't a preachy Christian who told everybody, "You've got to get right with God." My approach was to live out my faith as a witness.

"You love life too much," a coworker told me.

"Yeah, but I want to give my life to God and help others to love life."

Shortly after I resigned my job, Pastor Wells said, "I think it's time to ordain you." By that time I had met all the necessary requirements. The congregation of Union Baptist voted overwhelmingly in favor of my ordination. And just one year after I was ordained, Mariners' Temple called me to be their interim pastor.

Today I have a constant reminder of how God redirected my path: my church office overlooks the 155th Street bridge, where I finally surrendered to full-time ministry.

God had placed signposts along the way. He orchestrated events and people—even car wrecks and traffic jams—to bring me to that point. Once I knew where I was going, the next lesson I had to learn was knowing when to leave.

CHAPTER FIVE

Know When to Leave

My call into the ministry was incomprehensible to those who walked by sight. How could I leave such a lucrative position—I was one of only a handful of black television producers nationwide who could write my own ticket and go anywhere I wanted—to enter perhaps the least lucrative profession on earth?

I loved working in the television industry. Few people are able to obtain a great job in their desired field after graduation, yet I did. God had blessed me tremendously, but he was changing my season. And just as winter must move over when it is time for spring, the television industry had to take a hike as the pastoral ministry called my name.

Within one year of saying yes to the call of Christ, I was ordained in a church world that had originally told me it would take at least ten years. Reverend Ollie Wells, the one who encouraged me to answer God's call to preach, and the congregation

63

of Union Baptist warmly received me as a minister. They had loved Wilbert Johnson for forty years, and their love extended to his daughter.

The church that had nurtured me as a child helped to birth my ministry. I worked with the youth, led worship, read Scripture, preached, and taught. Other women in my seminary were not so fortunate. Most were not allowed to preach, or when they were, they had to preach from the floor, not from behind the pulpit. That would have been too controversial in the churches they served. In contrast, I was welcomed as Reverend Sujay. And while Pastor Wells was recovering from a heart attack, I took over many of the leadership responsibilities.

I also started working in the regional office of our denominational judicatory, the American Baptist Churches of Metropolitan New York. I did media and communications work for the denomination, and it was exciting to have the opportunity to utilize my television experience and skills for God's kingdom.

Working at the regional office brought me in contact with the many pastors who stopped by on business. When the pastors needed someone to fill in while they were on vacation, or they needed a speaker for a special event, they contacted the regional office. Because they had had the opportunity to get to know me personally, the issue of a woman minister didn't seem quite so threatening, and soon I was receiving invitations to fill pulpits on a regular basis.

In January 1983 I filled in for a pastor who was taking time off to visit his family in the Caribbean. The church was Mariners' Temple, the oldest Baptist church in Manhattan. When the pastor resigned a couple of months later, I asked one of my colleagues, who worked at the desk next to mine in the regional office, "Do you think they would consider a woman pastor?"

"They might," he said.

Since I was the last visiting minister to have filled the pulpit, Mariners' Temple asked me to fill in again. And on the first Sunday of March, exactly one year after my ordination, the congregation voted me in as interim pastor. My home church, Union Baptist, gave me a standing ovation when I announced Mariners' decision. My fellow seminarians (I was completing my senior thesis) went wild. They held a special service for me and presented me with a gift. Many of my pastoral colleagues encouraged me, although in the same breath they said, "Don't get your hopes up. It's too much to expect them to make you senior pastor."

My Mariners' Moment

Indeed, nothing looked very hopeful when I began my ministry as interim pastor at Mariners' Temple. In a once-beautiful old sanctuary that would seat eleven hundred people, only fifteen people were present. But I began to motivate them and encourage them to trust God for growth. We worked together. We met early in the mornings and handed out flyers in subway stations and at bus stops. The members started getting excited about church and inviting their friends and neighbors. In six months we had 150 people in church.

During those six months, the church continued to interview pastors. Finally they decided to quit looking. "We already have the pastor we want," the pulpit committee told the denominational office. "Reverend Johnson has been doing the work, and we want to vote her in as our pastor."

On Thursday, October 6, 1983, my name was formally submitted for a congregational vote. I was a nervous wreck. My mother and brother drove me to a restaurant downtown to wait while the church conducted its business meeting. We ordered coffee and dessert, but I found it impossible to eat.

After what seemed like an eternity, I spotted one of the officers coming into the restaurant. She was smiling broadly as she approached the table. "What is it? What was the vote?" I asked.

She wouldn't say. "You'll find out when we get there."

It must have gone in my favor, or surely she wouldn't be smiling, I thought. And then I had a moment of paranoia. *How can I tell if her smile is genuine?*

When we got to the church, there was no doubt about the outcome. The people were standing and cheering. Reverend Carl Flemister, the executive minister of our region, served as official spokesman. "Will you be the pastor of Mariners' Temple?" he asked.

I was so choked up, I couldn't answer. My mother was crying, and my brother was wiping his eyes too.

"You haven't answered us."

"Yes, of course. Yes!" I said firmly as I finally recovered my voice.

At age twenty-six I had been unanimously elected as Mariners' Temple's twenty-sixth pastor.

From Stressed Out to Burned Out

Mariners' was a wonderful place for a woman just leaving seminary to enter the ranks of the senior pastorate. It was raw and I was ready. The church needed energy and I had it. I needed a position where I could serve and God provided it. The Lord put us together to work miracles.

I placed before the people a vision of what God could do through us. As the congregation grew in numbers, so did their hope and expectation that God really would accomplish great things. The breakthrough came when we wanted to buy the building next door to the church; we had specific ministry plans for it. However, a $70,000 mortgage remained on the building, and we had only six weeks to raise the money or the opportunity would be lost.

It was primarily a low-income congregation. Most of our members lived in federally funded housing developments. But I challenged the people: "If we all bring what little money we have and put it together, God can multiply it." They gave generously, sacrificially. Some of my personal friends got behind the project. And against all odds, we raised $70,000 in six weeks. Getting the deed to that property was a turning point for the church and for the community: it was the first time black people had ever owned anything in that neighborhood.

Before long we turned our attention to buying the church building from the denomination. We managed to raise $90,000 and bought the church building. If nothing else happened in my season at Mariners', and a lot of good things did happen, people who had always lived with a could-not attitude learned that they really could. They soon memorized one of my favorite Bible verses: "I can do all things through Christ who strengthens me" (Phil. 4:13).

As I mentioned in Chapter 1, I was so stressed out by the end of my first year at Mariners' that I joked about needing an entire month off. I did start taking some time off, but I didn't make enough changes to relieve the stress. People's expectations were high, and mine were even higher. So I pushed myself to exceed everyone's expectations.

Eventually I burned out. After five years at Mariners' I was physically exhausted and emotionally spent. Burnout is a black hole of depression, a quagmire of emptiness. I had no desire to go to the church; I wanted to run in the other direction. I forced myself to go through the motions. My college experience in performing, along with God's grace, carried my pulpit ministry through those dark days when my preaching fire was nearly extinguished. God is faithful to his word—the gospel is still the gospel no matter how broken the vessel—so sinners still got saved and saints got inspired. But the inspirer desperately needed inspiration; the leader needed to be led.

The ministerial community operates under the motto "Never let them see you sweat." The pastor is supposed to have everything under control, so you can't share your problems with anyone. But what happens when the pastor needs to sweat?

I hit a wall that fifth year. It was worse than a runner's wall; it was a preacher's wall. I had peaked very fast. Because I was making history, the media were constantly in my face. I was the new "phenom," a black woman, in Chinatown, in a historic church that was about to die. And I helped revive it.

In five years we built the church from fifteen people to five hundred. We bought the church building and the building next door. A dying black church in Chinatown, led by a young, single woman going up against a system that said women weren't welcome, began to thrive. The price of that success, however, was enormous.

When I needed help recovering from burnout, I turned to inspirational books. Through the encouraging words of authors who had crossed this valley before me, and with the support of several sister-friends in the ministry, I began climbing out of the pit I had dug for myself.

Finding Wholeness

In confronting my burnout, I learned a valuable lesson that years later became the basis for one of the most dramatic sermons I ever preached.

The fifth chapter of John's Gospel relates the story of a man who was stuck in a predicament. He had been paralyzed for thirty-eight long, painful years. Like many other people who were sick or infirm, the man lay by the pool of Bethesda. The Bible says that periodically an angel would stir the waters, and "whoever stepped in first, after the stirring of the water, was made well of whatever disease he had" (John 5:4).

As I studied this incident, it began to dawn on me that his healing had been there all along, within his reach, yet he had not received it. When Jesus came on the scene, he asked one question: "Do you want to be made well?" (John 5:6). He did not ask, "How did you get in this condition?" He simply asked the man if he wanted to be made whole.

That was the question facing me: Did I want to be made whole? The question was not how I got stuck in my predicament. The question was not who was going to help me get out of it. The question was whether I really wanted to be whole. And if so, was I ready to help myself?

Just like the man by Bethesda's pool, I had not seen what I really needed. I could try to shift the blame and continue to criticize others, but doing that wouldn't bring healing. Doing that was the equivalent of lying by the pool. I had been operating in overdrive for so long that all I wanted to do was lie around somewhere. When I finally recognized that Jesus was asking me, "Do you want to be made whole?" I answered, "Yes, Lord!"

Finding wholeness required taking a long, hard look at myself. I had fallen into a trap that ensnares many of us who are called to Christian ministry, particularly when we're young in the ministry. I had gone overboard, thinking that working for the Lord meant giving myself away. I took the scriptural concept that "I must decrease, so that Christ may increase" to the extreme. I had decreased the attention I paid to myself. And I had done it in the name of the Lord, convincing myself that I was doing it for him.

I learned that God never intended anyone to be on call twenty-four hours a day, draining herself to the point that she was resentful or sick. If the leader is sick, how can she take care of the followers?

When the low fuel light comes on in your car, you can usually drive for a few more miles. The warning indicator reminds you to refuel; if you don't, you will run completely out of gas and your car will stop. My warning light had been on for years, but I had not stopped to refuel.

So I made some tough decisions. I asked myself, "How can I preserve myself so that I can reach the full potential the Lord desires for me?" I changed destructive patterns I had established and untangled myself from stressful situations. I started taking lunch breaks instead of working straight through the day. I distanced myself from some people who were dragging me down, not building me up. For example, one of my so-called friends felt compelled to share with me all the negative stories she heard about me in ministry circles. All that gossip was poison to my spirit. Since she didn't seem to be able to stop herself from passing it on, I decided she was not really my friend, and I quit seeing her.

I stopped being quite so available to my congregation. It was not that I did not care for them and their problems. It was a matter of recognizing that I could not solve them all at once. I made a rule that my home is not my office. I started screening my phone calls. I began setting boundaries.

One of the tough decisions I made, and one I got a lot of flak about, was setting a policy that I would do funerals only for members of our church. If I had tried to do funerals for everyone in the community, as I was being asked to do, I would have been preaching a funeral service seven days a week. Violence claimed many lives in our neighborhood, and life was hard there.

Gradually I was getting unstuck from my predicament. Like the man by Bethesda's pool, I quit lying around. I "took up my bed and walked." About seven years later, just before I left Mariners' Temple, I reenacted the Bethesda story for the congregation. I began my sermon lying down in the pulpit. I remained motionless for a long time, and then I looked up as Jesus asked me, "Do you want to be made whole?" Like the man who had been paralyzed for thirty-eight years, I danced around the question, making excuses for why my healing had not come.

Then I told the people how Jesus confronted the man at Bethesda, how he made the man confront himself. And as I struggled to get up from my prone position, I described how the strength came back into his legs when Jesus told him to get up and walk. People began to cry loudly.

"Somebody is here today," I said, "and you have been stuck in the same place for a long time. You really want to move from where you are, but you've been looking to others to do it for you. Jesus is asking you, 'Do you want your healing? Or are you content to stay where you are?'"

People started running to the altar, telling the Lord they wanted to change their lives. Several invited Jesus into their hearts that day. One couple who had been living together for a long time came up to me and said, "Pastor, we want to get married." A woman who had been unemployed for years admitted she had not really been looking for work. Her daughters, who were in high school, had never seen their mother stick with any job for an entire year. She said, "It's time for me to get up and do something with my life." The woman enrolled in college and graduated the same year as one of her daughters.

That message about the man at Bethesda was one of the highlights of my ministry at Mariners' Temple. I could preach it only after going through my own long, sometimes painful, process of getting unstuck from my predicament. Even today I have to be careful not to fall back into my old workaholic patterns. But I can assure you that it is possible to find wholeness, and it begins with asking yourself the question: "Do I want to be made whole?"

My Winter Season

The next couple of years were a winter season in my ministry. I replenished my physical, spiritual, and emotional resources, yet I still experienced a restlessness.

In my seventh year of pastoring I also served as a president's administrative fellow at Harvard University Divinity School. I was invited to stay at Harvard as an associate dean, but I felt the time just wasn't right to leave Mariners' Temple. Some difficulties had arisen within the congregation. To leave in the middle of a storm would have left the wrong perception, so I stayed. Gradually we identified the sources of the problems, and things began to stabilize again.

During that restless period, however, I first applied to be a White House fellow. The fellowship program brings together young leaders from professional communities across the United States to work at the executive level of government—with the president, the vice president, or a cabinet secretary—for one year. I had dreamed of this opportunity since I was fresh out of college, when I met a White House fellow while I was working for a TV station in Washington, D.C.

When I applied for the fellowship during the Bush administration, I was interviewed in Boston, the bastion of New England conservatism. Wearing a stylish purple suit, I walked confidently into a room full of interviewers dressed in cookie-cutter black business suits and a few navy blue blazers, which seemed almost daring by comparison. I immediately thought to myself, *Hmm. I don't think we're going to connect.* Although my interviews went well, it was obvious that I was a little too liberal and had a little too much pizzazz for that conservative crowd. I did make some good contacts, though, including President Bush's sister. We stayed in touch for a long time.

It was not my season to be in the White House. Instead, it was my season to fall in love, get married, and start a family. And what a wonderful time that was.

Recognizing the Seasons of Life

What a welcome sight the first buds of spring are each year. As brisk winds blow the snows away, we who are winter-weary anticipate the appearance of colorful blossoms and the trilling of songbirds once again.

In the same way that winter gives way to spring and summer ushers in fall, we go through seasons in our lives. I am relishing a spring season in my life right now, a time of new beginnings both personally and professionally. I feel reinvigorated as I encounter many "buds" and "blossoms," some opening up widely, others just waiting for a divine moment to reveal themselves. This spring season, however, follows a winter season in my life, a drab interval without growth or vitality.

This has probably happened to you too. Even when we have a clear direction, even when we reach our target destination, we sometimes find that God keeps us there only for a season. So we have to know where we're going in life, and we have to know when it's time to leave.

Sometimes we leave a difficult situation too soon, and we miss a blessing God had waiting for us because we didn't hold on. Other times we stay put when it's past time to leave; then we're in danger of stagnating spiritually and emotionally. Leaving too soon or staying too long can add tremendous stress to an already stressed-out life.

As I share how I recently made my staying-or-leaving decision, perhaps it will help you better understand how the Lord is working in your life. Not every season of your life will be springtime, of course. But knowing that a winter season is just that—a season—will help you remain where God wants you until it is time to move forward.

Seasons of Life

To everything there is a season,
A time for every purpose under heaven:
A time to be born,
    And a time to die;
A time to plant,
    And a time to pluck what is planted;
A time to kill,
    And a time to heal;
A time to break down,
    And a time to build up;
A time to weep,
    And a time to laugh;
A time to mourn,
    And a time to dance;

73

A time to cast away stones,
And a time to gather stones;
A time to embrace,
And a time to refrain from embracing;
A time to gain,
And a time to lose;
A time to keep,
And a time to throw away;
A time to tear,
And a time to sew;
A time to keep silence,
And a time to speak;
A time to love,
And a time to hate;
A time of war,
And a time of peace. (Eccl. 3:1–8)

We can demonstrably reduce our stress levels when we learn to understand the seasons of our lives. To do that, we must know ourselves. We must listen to our bodies not only intellectually but also emotionally and spiritually.

It is equally important to know God. Each day God is trying to tell us something. Each day we must listen. He instructed us to pray, "Give us this day our daily bread." We do not ask for an entire loaf at one time; we ask for *daily* bread, whatever we need to sustain and help us through that particular day.

Ask God to help you identify and understand the seasons in your life. Is this a time to move, or a time to stay put? Is this a time to work hard, or a time to rest and relax? "To everything there is a season."

My White House Season

After overcoming the restlessness I experienced in my seventh year of pastoral ministry, I stayed at Mariners' Temple another five years. And then, in my twelfth year, my season changed again. Just when you get to feeling comfortable, God will come along and rock your boat. He won't tip you over, but he will let you rock.

My first son, Samuel, was born in October 1992. After the presidential election in November, I began thinking about my dream of a White House fellowship again. The thought occurred to me that if I was ever going to do it, that would be the time. The incoming administration promised to be much more diverse and laid-back—my purple suit might even seem too stuffy for the young Clinton crowd—and interested in the issues that really motivated me.

I also wasn't getting any younger. To be a fellow in something always sounds like an internship, the kind of thing you need to do before you are too entrenched. I figured if I didn't do it while I was still in my thirties, I never would. So I decided to do all the paperwork for the application, send it in, pray, and see what happened.

That was the season for fulfilling my dream. In April 1993, seventeen White House fellows were selected nationwide, and I was one of them. Mariners' Temple allowed me to take a year's sabbatical. One of the things I had accomplished in twelve years was mentoring other women in ministry, so competent staff members were in place who could carry on the work in my absence. I could leave confident that the church was in capable hands.

In September 1993 I began working as a domestic policy advisor to President William J. Clinton. It was an outstanding year and provided everything I was looking for. I needed to be stretched, and it stretched me. I needed to be surrounded by other bright, young leaders who were success stories in their own rights, from a variety of disciplines and backgrounds, and it provided just that. It was humbling to recognize that I was not the only bright and shining star in the universe.

My year in the White House also helped me to answer some tough personal and theological questions. I thought I had political interests, and I questioned whether I should be using my gifts in that arena. But God reconfirmed to me that it is through pastoring, not politics, that I can most help people. That season might come someday, so I won't completely rule out an elected or appointed political office. Every time I think about it, however, God makes clear to me that the pulpit is where I'm supposed to be.

I had made a commitment to return to Mariners' after my year in the White House. In August 1994 I headed home.

You Can't Cross the Same River Twice

As I left Washington, some of my friends asked me, "How will you be able to make the adjustment? Can you really just go back and pick up where you left off?"

I didn't quite understand what they meant. "It's no big deal. I made a commitment; I'm going back," I said. I had given Mariners' my word I would return. To do anything else would have been less than honorable.

But when I returned, I discovered that it wasn't as easy as I had thought. Things had changed in my life, and the changes necessitated a new direction in my ministry.

For one thing, I was pregnant with our second child. When I had started my ministry at Mariners', I was in my twenties and single. I devoted every waking moment to building my ministry and growing the church. That had already changed dramatically, but it needed to change even more. I was still seriously short-changing my family. There were only so many hours in a day, so many days in a week, so many weeks in a month. And I was away from the people who meant the most to me more than I wanted to be.

I began to pray about how I could restructure my ministry to make more time for my family. I was determined that I would not miss out on seeing my children grow up. I did not want them to say someday, "I didn't know my mom. She was always out there helping other people, but she didn't have time to help me." My children were answers to prayer, and I wanted to be a good steward over the lives God had entrusted to my care.

In addition to the time demands, I realized that Mariners' and I had grown differently. Their needs no longer seemed to mesh with my gifts. I was frustrated because I had talents and abilities that I felt weren't being used. My vision has always been big, and it had grown even larger. I wanted to do more, to change the world. The people at Mariners' and I seemed to be going in different directions.

The restlessness that had plagued me in my seventh year of pastoring came back, and I began to evaluate whether it was a sign that God was about to change my season. When we are seeking signs from God, we sometimes find them in unusual places. He seldom sends angels or earthquakes, but the still, small voice of the Spirit can speak to our hearts unmistakably— just as he spoke to Elijah after the wind, the earthquake, and the fire (1 Kings 19:11–12).

One of my signs came from television. A guest on *Oprah* was talking about a book by Alice Walker titled *Same River Twice*. Its thesis, as she described it, was that you can never really go back to the same waters. Not only are you no longer the same, but neither are the waters you left. The current has changed. The elements of nature have affected the stream. When you return, although it appears the same, it really is a different river and you are a different person. Therefore, you cannot cross the same river twice.

That described my situation. Washington had not changed me. I had been changing before I left; Washington was merely the place God gave me to provide some distance so that I could arrive at an unemotional decision. I was grateful for that distance. Most people have to decipher these changes while trying to function in the middle of the very situation they're questioning.

Mariners' was a wonderful beginning to my ministry. I will always be grateful to God, and grateful to the congregation, for the years I spent there. I do not consider a single moment wasted. In fact, it was a blessing.

In a sense, Mariners' was my spiritual boot camp. The basic training I received there laid the foundation for my ministry today. In fact, the two-hundred-year history of Mariners' as a mission church points to it as a learning station for new ministers coming out of seminary. Out of the twenty-five ministers who had preceded me, twenty-four had been student ministers or placed there by the denomination. I had stayed twice as long as most of them.

When I finally left, I was a seasoned pastor, and Mariners' Temple was a seasoned ministry.

Prayer for Direction

Dear God, I am often overwhelmed by the decisions I must make for my life. Help me to relax and realize that when one door shuts, you have already opened another. I am learning that each difficulty is your opportunity. I am learning to flow with you. Teach me to look, listen, hear, and move according to your perfect will.

Order my steps in your Word, dear Lord. Send me to the places you want me to go. Match my gifts with the right situation. I feel I am ready to make a move, but I will not and cannot move without you. I love you, Lord, and I know that when I get to where you will have me to be, I will serve with great joy and gladness. In the meantime, teach me to serve you where I am now with great joy, until I am ready to go where you are taking me.

Help me to discern the seasons of life, dear Lord. Hold me back if it's time to stay put, and prod me if it's time to leave. I want to live so that what I desire for myself is the same as what you desire for me. Amen.

A New Springtime for Ministry

As I prayed for confirmation about leaving, God's hand began to move in my life. While I was in labor with my second son, Christopher, in May 1995, the Lord revealed to me that I was going to give spiritual birth to a new ministry. I was so preoccupied with giving physical birth that I could not clearly determine God's direction at first.

But every time I looked at my newborn son, I heard God's voice whisper, "New birth." At the time, Mariners' was helping an associate launch a new church. "Lord, does 'new birth' mean helping her?" I asked.

"No, you are going to build a new church," he said.

In June 1995 I traveled to Virginia for the Hampton Ministers' Conference. It was always the highlight of my year, and I didn't want to miss it, even though it was so soon after Christopher's birth. And having a few hours alone on an airplane allowed me to have some quiet time with God. During the flight, the Lord began to give me a vivid picture of the new birth he had in store for me. He gave me the name of the new church, the neighborhood, even the bylaws. I saw the people who would be coming. I saw the kind of ministry I would be doing. I wrote down everything I was seeing and hearing in the Spirit. None of it resembled, even slightly, where I had been. God was definitely doing a new thing in me and through me.

By that time I knew that if I stayed at Mariners', I would be financially and occupationally comfortable but spiritually and emotionally depleted because I would be missing God's new birth. But leaving meant taking a risk, moving by faith to a new place, and starting a new ministry from the ground up.

When I made the decision to venture into new waters with God, he led me step by step and confirmed every single decision. He brought the right people and situations into my life to let me know without any doubt that I was doing the right thing. God even gave me the benefit of time, allowing me to begin to build the new ministry while I was still pastoring at Mariners'.

I went to our denominational leaders and presented my plan to start a new ministry, Bronx Christian Fellowship, in the community that nurtured me as I was growing up. I shared with them the need for new birth in my old neighborhood, the Yankee Stadium area. They gave their blessing—reluctantly at first, but I got the green light to proceed.

In September 1995 we launched a Thursday lunch-hour service, meeting in a rented church facility. I had been doing a Wednesday lunch-hour service at Mariners' that was quite successful and attracted many Wall Street workers. Our ministry team passed out flyers announcing the new service, and on Thursday, September 21, three hundred people showed up for the first meeting. That is not normal for launching a new ministry. But God is not normal; he is spectacular!

The Bronx ministry started out so successfully that many people were coming to the Lord. I was trying to direct them to other churches, but people kept saying, "No, you're our pastor. We don't want to go to another church." After about three months we added a Tuesday evening service, which met in the basement of a museum.

Even though I was serving two congregations—both Mariners' and Bronx Christian Fellowship—preaching five times weekly, and trying to hold it all together, my inner peace and joy increased. I regained my momentum. I was not burning out; I was on fire for God.

Higher Ground

I'm pressing on the upward way,
New heights I'm gaining ev'ry day;
Still praying as I'm onward bound,
"Lord, plant my feet on higher ground."
Chorus:
Lord, lift me up and let me stand,
By faith, on heaven's tableland;
A higher plane than I have found;
Lord, plant my feet on higher ground.

My heart has no desire to stay
Where doubts arise and fears dismay;
Though some may dwell where these abound,
My prayer, my aim is higher ground.

I want to live above the world,
Though Satan's darts at me are hurled;
For faith has caught the joyful sound,
The song of saints on higher ground.

"Higher Ground" is another hymn text by Reverend Johnson Oatman Jr. In his late thirties this businessman-preacher started writing gospel hymns, and he averaged writing four or five hymns each week for the next thirty years—never earning more than a dollar each for them.

The words of this song are priceless to me, though. I'm learning "to live above the world" or, as I call it, "living above the stress and the mess." The theme song of a once-popular TV sitcom said, "I'm movin' on up, to the East Side, to a deluxe apartment in the sky-y-y." Forget that East Side high-rise— I'm movin' on up to higher ground.

Broke but Blessed

In June 1996 it was time to finally cut loose from Mariners'. We had established a solid base for the new ministry with about 150 members. In the first year we saw more than two hundred people give their lives to Christ.

Most of our members are previously unchurched African-American and Latino professionals. The church is in an established, working-class neighborhood with many intact families. Our theme as a congregation is Celebrating the Family.

I am certainly celebrating my family. What I had asked God for—more time with my family—I now have. The church is just four blocks from my home. I can take Samuel to school in the morning and pick him up on my way home. The baby-sitter can bring Chris by the office any time. My husband's office is ten minutes away—just a short cab ride or one subway stop.

More than two hours' daily commuting time is gone. I did not realize just how stressful that trip down FDR Drive was until I didn't have to make it anymore. Most evenings I am home by six o'clock. I am a "new and improved" pastor with much more energy to tackle problems and find solutions.

While I am earning less money than I ever have, I am enjoying life more. Ron and I laugh and say, "Well, we may be broke, but we're blessed." The money will come later; the peace we have now.

Today I counsel many people who are wrestling with the issue of knowing when to leave. Some of them feel stuck where they are. As they speak, I often find that clear signals have been there for a while, and the decision to leave has already been made at a subconscious level; they simply need confirmation. Sometimes I have them repeat what they have just said (as Doris did with me all those years ago), or I repeat what I heard them say. Perhaps they lack confidence in their ability to garner the resources needed, or they are worried about what others would say.

I have learned that "wherever God guides, he provides." You may not have the same income the first few months, or you may skip a vacation or two you planned. But once you start to see the signs of change, once God starts to rock your boat, that is the time to start planning for your next move. Start putting money away before the rainy day comes. Store up your spiritual energy. Begin to have a focused prayer time about upcoming changes.

Invite others to be prayer partners with you. Keep a prayer journal, and record what God is saying to you. In time you'll be able to go back through the pages of your journal and see where the signs are pointing. Believe in God. Believe in yourself. The Lord will not place you where you are not ready. But if you are ready, then enjoy the ride.

If you want to be too blessed to be stressed, you need to know where you're going and know when to leave. But you also need to learn when to go forward and when to just relax and go with the flow.

CHAPTER SIX

Go
Forward

In the 1960s a remnant of country life clung to the corner of Fish Avenue and Eastchester Road in the northeast Bronx. Eastchester Presbyterian Church occupied a small white frame building on a large plot of grass, an island of green firmly anchored in a sea of concrete and asphalt. Eastchester's lawn was a welcome sight in the middle of urban life and the setting for picnics and pageants, nativity scenes and neighborhood gatherings.

My mom and dad and my brother, Ronald, and I had moved from 144th Street in Harlem to 213th Street in the Bronx. We were integrating the community and the church; most of the families at Eastchester were Italian. They received us graciously, and this church, which was small in structure but large in love, was one place I never felt any class or race or gender differences.

Reverend Millard Farrell made the Bible come alive for the neighborhood children. He wanted us to be able to articulate Christ, and he accomplished that by bringing vivid lessons from

Scripture. Reverend Farrell taught the Bible intensely. He also provided an environment where young people could develop their gifts and flourish in God's kingdom.

In junior church, among other kids our own age, we learned to sing hymns and participate in the leadership of the service. And for every holiday or special occasion we put on a pageant or performed a drama. We didn't follow a script some adult had dreamed up either; the children wrote and produced and acted in the reenactments of Bible stories. Our parents helped make the costumes and props, but we were the creators and stars.

Drama was a key to changing my life. It planted a seed in me that blossomed into a love for performing and producing. It also planted in me a love for God's Word. As a child, I was especially drawn to Bible stories about spiritual leaders and, of course, stories about women.

Now I know why. Today I am a woman whom God has called to lead his people. Most of my sermons center on these same biblical heroes and she-roes, with a contemporary flair. I'm the pastor trying to make the Bible come alive for men, women, and children, and what a joy that is.

The Bible's Real-Life Stories

Scripture presents a wealth of stories of salvation, hope, and deliverance. The Word shows us a man or woman of God so that we can see the parallels in our lives—so that we can see how people trusted God, overcame their struggles, galvanized themselves and others, and received their blessings.

Some familiar Bible characters went through extraordinary circumstances, such as surviving a flood, like Noah, or living in the belly of a whale, like Jonah. Many women also had supernatural experiences. For Mary, the mother of Jesus, to have conceived supernaturally is a once-in-history experience.

But all of those people were real, living in a real world, facing the same stresses and challenges we face today. They struggled with ethnic and racial problems. They battled financial problems and family crises. They lost battles and won wars. Kings were crowned and enemies brought low. Men and women fulfilled grand callings and muddled through mundane tasks. The Bible is filled with real-life stories, and that's why it has had tremendous appeal for so many centuries.

Two of my favorite biblical characters, Moses and Deborah, are in the Old Testament. They were daring and caring. Each led a group of people who had gotten to a certain point in their journey and then were struck with a paralysis of fear. Yet, despite the fear, they took their people forward.

Moses Went Forward

I am a woman on the move. I think it must be in my blood. From my earliest years, I have been traveling by land, air, and sea. I love movement, and I relish being around people and things that move.

One thing God has taught me is that movement needs to be in a forward direction. God will let us run around in circles, like Israel did around Mount Sinai, but he really desires us to move forward to our promised land. Forward movement is empowering. But sometimes people have to be strengthened and taught before they can make their decision to go forward.

That's what Moses discovered when God called him to lead his people out of Egypt. The Exodus is a wonderful story about leadership, impatience, discipline, liberation, and God's promises.

On his journey to the promised land, Moses found himself facing the Red Sea with a mumbling and grumbling people. It was amazing how God had used Moses to be the liberator for the children of Israel when they were entangled in slavery. He had come from an oppressive background, but God's grace—and a little heavenly strategic planning—kept Moses from death as a child and transformed him into a leader as an adult.

When Moses became their leader, he learned that the people of Israel had developed a callousness. They had grown comfortable with their enslavement and oppression. Yet God, who cannot tolerate oppression, wanted them to go forward. Moses, being a man of God, also wanted them to go forward. You can't be an effective leader and hold people in stagnation; the very nature of leadership calls for movement.

Through a series of miracles, God had led his people out of bondage, under the leadership of Moses. Now they were at the Red Sea, and the Egyptians were pursuing them. They were at an uncomfortable crossroads. Dr. Martin Luther King Jr. once said, "The measure of a man [or a woman, I would add] is not where he [or she] stands at moments of comfort, but rather at moments of challenge and controversy."[1] That's exactly where Moses and the children of Israel were, caught in a moment of challenge and controversy. The sea was in front of them, and the enemy was behind them. They had nowhere to turn.

We all know how the story ends. God parted the Red Sea, and Moses led the people forward to the promised land. But even after that dramatic miracle, many of the people did not want to go forward. They grumbled and complained: "Why did you bring us here, Moses? We should have stayed in Egypt. We're just going to die out here in the wilderness. Why did we ever leave?" They wanted to go back to slavery rather than go forward to God's blessing.

Going forward when others want to remain in the past is challenging. It often involves risk. Responding to God's command to go forward can be a stress-filled call. To help others go forward is even more difficult. But when God speaks, we must go forward.

Miriam's Song

When Pharaoh's horses, chariots and horsemen went into the sea, the Lord brought the waters of the sea back over them, but the Israelites walked through the sea on dry ground. Then Miriam the prophetess, Aaron's sister, took a tambourine in her hand, and all the women followed her, with tambourines and dancing. Miriam sang to them:

"Sing to the LORD,
for he is highly exalted.
The horse and its rider
he has hurled into the sea." (Ex. 15:19–21 NIV)

Songs of celebration after a victory in battle were common in Old Testament times. Moses composed a lengthy poem (Ex. 15:1–18) commemorating God's deliverance of the Israelites from the Egyptians. He probably read this hymn of praise to the assembled people, and then Miriam led them in singing the chorus.

I use Miriam's example as an illustration of the role of women in ministry. We're not out to take the place of the brothers; the sisters just want to help complete the song.

Deborah Went Forward

Deborah is my favorite biblical woman because she stepped in when the men could not handle what was going on. The fourth and fifth chapters of Judges tell Deborah's story. She was the judge, or ruler, of Israel at a time of national crisis. Jabin, the Canaanite king, was bullying Israel, and his army, commanded by Sisera, was hemming them in. Sisera had cruelly oppressed the Israelites for twenty years.

One day Deborah sent for Barak, the commander of Israel's army. She said to him, "Hasn't the Lord God already commanded you to deploy troops at Mount Tabor? Why haven't you done it?" The Bible doesn't come right out and say it, but Barak was afraid. He had heard God's command to go forward, but he lacked the courage.

"Take ten thousand men with you," Deborah said, "and go against Jabin's chariots at the Kishon River. The Lord has promised to deliver Sisera into your hands."

Barak's reply shows he was shaking in his boots. "I'll go if you go," he said. "But if you ain't goin', I ain't goin'." (That's from the Sujay translation.)

Deborah was cool and confident. She knew she was called to lead the people forward. So she said, "I'll gladly go with you, Barak. But there will be no glory for you, for the Lord will give Sisera into the hand of a woman."

I'll fast-forward to the end of the story. Deborah went into battle with Barak, and the Lord gave them a great victory over the Canaanites. Sisera escaped from the battle and fled to the tent of an ally. While he slept, Jael, the wife of his ally, hammered a tent peg into Sisera's temple. She was the woman who got the credit for destroying Israel's chief enemy.

Let's look now at some of the principles we can learn from Deborah's life. We will discover a biblical role model who was too blessed to be stressed.

Living Above the Stress and the Mess

As the first female judge of Israel, Deborah ruled at a particularly stressful time. Sisera's soldiers were closer than they had ever been. Fear had paralyzed the nation, even the commander of the army. The people were under attack and needed wise counsel. Deborah was prepared to offer it.

One of the first things we see in Scripture is that she chose her place wisely: "Now Deborah, a prophetess, the wife of Lapidoth, was judging Israel at that time. And she would sit under the palm tree of Deborah between Ramah and Bethel in the mountains of Ephraim. And the children of Israel came up to her for judgment" (Judg. 4:4–5).

She sat in a holy place, between Ramah and Bethel. Rather than running back and forth from one city to the other, she sat between them and let the people come to her. Already the text suggests she was a good time manager. Many of us are under severe stress because we are not good stewards of our time. We pile more onto our proverbial plates than we can ever handle. We expect too much of ourselves, and many, particularly those in public life, try to live up to other people's expectations. That adds to the pressure and leads to stress—and may prevent us from going forward when God calls us.

Deborah knew how to live above the stress and the mess. She was aware of how terrible the situation was for Israel, yet she did not concentrate on the terror. Nor did she walk out on her people at the very time she was needed. A good leader does not quit. She may take a break, but she does not exit.

When others see calamity, the woman of God sees calm. A mature leader will have been through moments similar to the ones experienced by those she is leading. God then brings spiritual recall to the memory of the leader, and she is able to give words of wisdom. That's who Deborah was: God's wise woman, God's leader. Deborah hung in there. After hearing God's word—hearing that it was indeed her battle—she led the troops forward into victory.

Choosing Your Battles

Another lesson we learn from Deborah's story is that it's important to know that not every battle is your battle. Nor is every time your time. When your time comes, and you are prepared, victory will happen.

This is especially important for women in the workplace because we often are assigned tasks we haven't asked for, or we are placed in leadership roles we haven't sought. With so many vital issues out there to be embraced, we must carefully and prayerfully determine which one, if any, we are able and called to handle.

As a woman in ministry, I hear from people all the time who want me to jump on their bandwagon. There are many movements—women's rights, civil rights, parachurch ministry, megachurch ministry—all asking for my time and attention. All these issues are significant, and I understand that women and men in these movements helped pave the way for me to be where I am today.

But I also understand that what I am called to handle, what God has gifted me to handle, is different from the other movements. God didn't call me to all those issues. He called me to preach the gospel. He called me to be a pastor, to feed and to lead his flock. I must be selective as to how I will use my time, my influence, and my pulpit. A wise woman understands that she cannot do everything, but she can do something. A wise woman chooses her battles.

When I graduated, I was one of the first women, if not the first, out of my entire seminary to be elected as a senior pastor of a black Baptist church. My new position created a major stir around the school, the city, and even the nation. More than one thousand people, including two dozen reporters, attended my installation. Before long, many visitors were coming to see this new phenomenon.

For the first year or so I was swamped with interviews, and our church people learned to ignore television cameras and reporters with microphones during worship services. One particular day, a journalist asked me about inclusive language. "When you preach," she said, "you refer to God as *he* and *our Father*. Doesn't that bother you? Wouldn't you prefer to change all the masculine pronouns and references in hymns and in Scripture to the feminine or to a non-gender-specific term?"

"No," I said. "In the black church tradition, Father God is a very comfortable image; you will hear it often. Many of my members grew up in the depression era or the war era when men were absent from the home. Many homes today do not have a male figure, and children need that. So it is important to understand God as our Father.

"But more than that, my presence in the pulpit makes a statement. It's historic. For more than two hundred years my denomination has not had a black woman in leadership in the pulpit. By my being the best leader I can be, people will have to see God and one another in new ways. I believe my presence in the pulpit as a woman speaks louder than any feminine pronoun ever can."

I'm not offended by people who take up this issue. Scholars raise these questions and challenge each of us to examine the character and nature of God and our understanding of God's Word; that is important. The total mission of some people is to change the language of the church, but the Lord opened a major door just for me to be there. It was not my issue to change all of the hymns. I knew I would have other battles to prioritize.

My answer seemed to satisfy the reporter as well as those trying to get me to join the inclusive language campaign. It was the end of the story and the end of the discussion. Nobody dismissed me because I took a stand. In fact, more people began to respect me because I stood for something. And it alleviated a lot of stress that would have arisen had I taken on that particular issue. Today many denominations insist on using inclusive language, but that was not the case in the 1980s.

Preaching was and is my gift, and I knew that when I started my ministry. Through my sermons, my life experiences as a woman, and the illustrations I used from a female point of view, people had to look at Bible texts in exciting new ways. I preached about biblical women in the first person, dramatically becoming those she-roes in the pulpit. In my early ministry I used my dramatic training to bring to life biblical women—Deborah, Miriam, Ruth, Naomi, and the woman with the issue of blood. No man could have preached those sermons the way I did because I could associate certain feelings with those characters that no man could have ever experienced.

That was my battle. And that was the plan for my ministry.

Making a Plan

Another lesson we learn from Deborah's life is that she had a plan. It was a plan of action not only for Israel's survival but also for her own. She had achieved a pace and a lifestyle that were comfortable for her. To get stressed out just because the situation was stressful would have defeated Deborah before she had a chance to defeat Sisera's army.

As a prophetess, Deborah knew God's faithfulness to his promises. She had sought God's plan for her people, so she was able to declare that plan confidently to Barak: "Take ten thousand men from the tribes of Naphtali and Zebulun, and deploy them at Mount Tabor." Deborah did not send her troops into battle without having a battle plan.

It is not enough to choose our issues carefully; we must also be clear about how much energy will be necessary. We must properly plan our course of action. Jesus also emphasized the importance of planning and marshaling our resources: "For which of you, intending to build a tower, does not sit down first and count the cost, whether he has enough to finish it—lest, after he has laid the foundation, and is not able to finish, all who see it begin to mock him" (Luke 14:28–29).

Do you want to be too blessed to be stressed? Then choose your issue carefully, if you have one, and don't try to fight every battle. Leave some work for others to do. Include God in your plan of action. And remember the following four Ds from Deborah's example.

Deborah's Song

On that day Deborah and Barak son of Abinoam sang this song:

"When the princes in Israel take the lead,
when the people willingly offer themselves—
praise the LORD!

"Hear this, you kings! Listen, you rulers!
　　I will sing to the LORD, I will sing;
　　I will make music to the LORD, the God of Israel. . . .
"In the days of Shamgar Son of Amath,
　　in the days of Jael, the roads were abandoned;
　　travelers took to winding paths.
Village life in Israel ceased,
　　ceased until I, Deborah, arose,
　　arose a mother in Israel.
When they chose new gods,
　　war came to the city gates,
and not a shield or spear was seen
　　among forty thousand in Israel.
My heart is with Israel's princes,
　　with the willing volunteers among the people.
　　Praise the LORD! . . .
"So may all your enemies perish, O LORD!
　　But may they who love you be like the sun
　　when it rises in its strength."
Then the land had peace forty years.
(Judg. 5:1–3, 6–9, 31 NIV)

Known as the Song of Deborah, this is another song commemorating a national victory. Many scholars believe it was
written by Deborah, and it is one of the oldest poems in the
Bible.

Note that after Deborah led her people to victory, they
enjoyed peace for forty years. That's what happens when you
go forward with God's help.

Deborah's Four Ds

I have identified four Ds that stand for four principles in Deborah's life. These principles will help you in your quest to move
forward and be rid of some of the stress in your life.

Dare

The first D stands for *dare*. Deborah dared to have a distinctive leadership style. She dared to be herself. She created a special place to do her business, a place that provided serenity and soothed her spirit. The Bible says that she sat under the palm tree between Ramah and Bethel.

Never before in history had anyone ruled from under a palm tree, but Deborah dared to do it. I imagine the outdoor setting was soothing for her. I love to travel to warm climates where palm trees abound. Sitting under those trees is both relaxing and exhilarating for me. For whatever reasons, Deborah chose that location to rule the nation. The spot became so well known that throughout the following centuries it was called the Palm Tree of Deborah.

Recently I brought a work of art back from a trip to Egypt. One of my office assistants overheard me telling someone how much I admired it. I said I was going to hang it in the waiting area of the church. Later she told me, "Pastor, you should surround *yourself* with beautiful things. You're always helping others to feel comfortable. Why not make yourself comfortable as well? Put that painting in your office or your home study where you can enjoy it every day."

I dared to take her advice, and now this favorite piece is hanging in my office. This painting, on Egyptian papyrus, presents the Pyramids in delicately beautiful colors; it also has palm trees. Like Deborah, I now sit and counsel under the palm trees.

Dare to have your surroundings reflect who you are. You do not have to be poured into someone else's mold. Dare to make your mark. Use colors and styles that bring you joy. Dare to be yourself.

When I first began my pastoral ministry, there were virtually no women my age as role models. Most of the women in seminary with me were older; in fact, their children were my age. I had no one to pattern myself after. At first I thought I had to wear dark suits with very long skirts all the time. I was afraid to wear slacks or any of the clothing with some dazzle that I really enjoyed. My pastor and my mother finally sat me down and asked, "What are you comfortable wearing? Why shouldn't you wear fire-engine reds and bright blues and purples, or even slacks, if that's what you want?"

When I became a mother, I dared to make another change in my ministry. Most children sit with their mothers in the church service. When my son saw all the other kids sitting with their mothers but his mommy stood behind the pulpit, it didn't compute. How could I explain to a twelve-month-old child that Mommy couldn't hold him or kiss him or tend to his needs because I had to preach?

I devised a strategy for helping Samuel cope with this problem. I divided the regular tithe from special offerings and started taking up two collections during the service. The first offering is a traditional one, where the ushers pass the plates to the people in their pews. During the second offering, the choir sings while the congregation brings special gifts to the front of the church, passing in front of the pulpit. As the processional starts, whoever is sitting with my son brings him to my seat on the dais. Samuel climbs on my lap, hangs on my neck, and for a few minutes has my undivided attention. When the last of the congregants reach the front, the baby-sitter on assignment retrieves my happy boy.

Dare to come up with a creative solution to your problem. So what if it has never been done that way before. Does it work for you? Does it honor God? Then dare to do it! *Can I get a witness?*

Discipline

The second D is for *discipline*. I believe that one of the reasons Deborah ruled from under the palm tree is that she had to make disciplined decisions about where she could and could not be effective.

We are called to be disciples. Notice how close that word is to the word *discipline*. Disciples should be disciplined people. Some women are spread so thin, trying to make every appointment, every program, every social event, until they're not effective at anything.

I've been there. Sometimes I couldn't enjoy where I was because my mind was on the next place I was supposed to be. It's partly a time management issue, but it is also a discipline issue. I had to discipline my spirit—and my ego—to realize that I did not have to be everywhere and that some things really could go on without me.

Early in my ministry, one of my best girlfriends taught me a valuable lesson in self-discipline. Alexis and I had been friends since my early days in the television industry. Every time she moved up, she made sure I got considered for the job she was leaving. And I usually got it.

I've always traveled in and out of Washington, D.C. I love the city. On one of my trips, Alexis invited me to have lunch with her at one of the capital's classiest restaurants. It should have been a relaxing time for two old friends to catch up on each other's life while pampering ourselves with fine cuisine in an elegant atmosphere.

But Alexis could tell from my limited conversation that I was frazzled. That was one of the reasons she wanted to see me. She had heard I was doing way too much, and she loved me enough to confront me about it.

"What's wrong with you, Sujay? Your mind is somewhere else today," she said.

"I'm sorry. I've been in so many meetings this week that I guess I'm all talked out."

"You're trying to do entirely too much, aren't you?"

"Well, there's an awful lot to do," I said, somewhat defensively. "I'm the pastor, you know. And when the people need counseling, I can't very well send them away."

"No, but you don't have to see them all at once. How many counseling sessions do you usually have each day?"

"Oh, it varies." I hesitated before telling her just how many. "Between seven and ten probably."

"Every day?" she asked, her eyebrows rising and her mouth dropping open in surprise. "On top of all the administrative stuff?"

"Yeah." I smiled wearily. "Welcome to my world."

"Your world is insane," Alexis said. "You can't keep that up." She looked as if she didn't know whether to shake some sense into me or console me. "Tell me what a typical day is like for you."

I told her about leaving home before 7:00 A.M., driving more than an hour in heavy traffic, hunting a parking place, then finding four or five people lined up outside my office waiting to see me. Plus, I would have six or seven meetings on the day's agenda, requests for interviews, calls from pastors wanting me to preach a special service, and somewhere in there I had to find time to prepare sermons for four services a week.

"You've got to cut back somewhere, Sujay. Why do you have to see so many people every day? Try seeing only three or four."

"No, no, no. I can't do that. They need me. I'm the pastor."

"Look, you can't solve everybody's problems all at once. Most of the problems will still be there the next day. But *you* won't if you keep this up."

Like a good little workaholic, I resisted her. I don't know why workaholics always resist efforts to help them slow down, but they do. And at the time, I was very driven and wanted to prove myself as a pastor.

Alexis kept after me, and I finally said, "Okay, okay, I'll try cutting down."

Then she said, "Discipline yourself to make time for your own spirit." It was hard for me to admit, but that was something I had not done. My body was running so fast, my spirit couldn't catch up. Thank God for a girlfriend who knew me that well.

The next week I cut my schedule in half. I published in the church bulletin the hours I would be available to the congregation for counseling—three hours on Tuesday and three hours on Wednesday—and asked them to make an appointment first. A few of them resisted initially because they were spoiled by a long-standing open-door policy. But my stress was lightened considerably by not having to face a lineup outside my office every morning. And my counseling improved. I was in much better condition to listen when I wasn't so bone weary.

Determination

The next D is for *determination*. Once Deborah knew she had God's nod of approval, she prepared herself to go into battle. When Barak said, "I'll go if you'll go with me," Deborah did not push him aside and try to fight the battle by herself. She knew God had promised victory, and she was determined to be a winner. But she also knew that God's plan involved a winning team: Deborah was the nation's leader, Barak was the commander of the army, and ten thousand soldiers were appointed to the battle.

Be determined to win your battles, but also make sure you have the help you need. Understanding—and acting on—this point is especially important for pastors and church leaders. Too many Christians are what I call Palm Sunday Christians: they cheer you on Sunday, but where are they five days later when the crowd is ready to crucify you? Initial enthusiasm for a project can fade quickly; surround yourself with committed Christians who will stick with you through the tough spots.

Diet

The final D stands for *diet*. This refers to our intake of food and to whatever else we take into our bodies. The thoughts we allow to occupy our minds are important, and we often have to make a conscious decision not to entertain destructive thoughts. Yet some people feed on mental junk food. Negative clutter fills their minds until they are down on life in general and themselves in particular.

You have to learn that you cannot listen to everyone. Not everyone is there to strengthen you. You cannot win victories when you listen to defeatist conversation, whether it is coming from another person or whether you are talking to yourself.

Deborah was clear on what she allowed to enter her thought pattern. This woman of God cut off the conversation about fear and losing the battle. She rose to the occasion and did what she set out to do: help Israel win the victory. She dared to be different and dared to be herself. She disciplined her time and her spirit. She was determined to win the battle because she knew she had heard from God.

I'll Go Where You Want Me to Go

It may not be on the mountain's height,
Or over the stormy sea;
It may not be at the battle's front
My Lord will have need of me;
But if by a still, small voice He calls
To paths I do not know,
I'll answer, dear Lord, with my hand in Thine,
I'll go where You want me to go.

Chorus:
I'll go where You want me to go, dear Lord,
O'er mountain, or plain, or sea;
I'll say what You want me to say, dear Lord,
I'll be what You want me to be.

Few of us will ever be called to lead a nation in crisis, as Moses and Deborah were. Yet we can have an untold influence on our families, our neighborhoods, our schools, or our workplaces by demonstrating a willingness to go forward when God leads.

Hearing from God

Both biblical examples we've looked at, Moses and Deborah, listened to and heard from God. Going forward is the response of God's people when they have taken the time to hear him.

Recently I had an opportunity that one of my preacher-mentors describes as "an embarrassment of riches." Many people feel they have no choices in life. I suddenly found myself with too many. I had to put all of Deborah's Ds into action and come up with a personal victory for my life.

Here I was, a prosperous pastor (in terms of having a flourishing new congregation), a wife, the mother of two healthy and energetic little boys, and a chaplain for the New York City Police Department. By anyone's standards that is a very full load. Then a seat became vacant for a local political office, a very influential position that would be appropriate for someone with my background and experience.

When I was first approached about running, I was flattered. *I really could win*, I told myself. *Then I could help all the others I've wanted to help in the past.*

Flattery can be a contributor to stress, for more often than not we are listening to the hearts' desires of others. I told those who asked me that I would pray about it, and I did. This was an act of *discipline*. I also invited others to join me in prayer and fasting because this decision would impact my ministry and my family. This was my *diet*: I could not listen to everyone; I had to hear from God.

After three days of prayer and fasting, I specifically asked God what he wanted for my life at this time (I was *determined* to do his will), and I revisited some of the things I had wanted for myself at this stage of my life (I *dared* to be my own person). I heard God clearly. His answer was no. This was not my time, not my place.

God had given me everything I had asked for the previous year: a ministry in my home neighborhood, more time with my husband and children, and time to think through ideas as a pastor. If I had jumped on this new opportunity, I would have undone what God had just done for me. This was not my season to hold a political office; this was my season to thank God for answered prayer—and to go forward with my ministry.

I encourage you to go forward also. But if you are too blessed to be stressed, you will understand that there are times when you just have to go with the flow. And sometimes you will need to stop completely. Let's learn now how to recognize God's traffic signs.

CHAPTER SEVEN

Go with the Flow

Dropping my suitcase to the floor, I flipped the dead bolt on the door behind me. After several days on the road, I was glad to be home where I could relax. I just knew things would be in order. I would get my hugs, hit the bed, and thank God for traveling mercies.

Instead I found dirty dishes piled in the kitchen sink and toys scattered in the living room. I followed a trail of socks and shoes into the bedroom, thinking, *It looks as if I've been gone for three years, not three days.*

I both laughed and groaned at the sight awaiting me in the bedroom. "Who left the spareribs in the bed?" I wondered out loud.

At the sound of my voice, two bubbly little boys came running to greet me. I did get plenty of hugs, but the relaxing evening I had anticipated was busted.

Does this scene sound familiar to you?

No matter how busy I get or how many out-of-town trips I make, I'm still the mom. I'm adjusting to the fact that every time I return from a trip it takes about a week for my household to get back to normal.

It's not always the big things in life that overwhelm us. Sometimes it's the accumulation of little things—the spareribs-in-the-bed episodes—that can leave us frayed around the edges.

One of the lessons I'm learning is that there are times when it's necessary to loosen up and go with the flow. If a tree battered by the wind does not bend, it will break. The same is true for us. When the unanticipated happens—and it will—we have to be flexible.

Don't Try to Swim Upstream

When learning to swim in running water, you have to find the flow of the water and go with it. Swimming upstream causes exhaustion. Downstream will take you rapidly to your destination. And so it is with life.

The fact that many women are now entering jobs and vocations we have never had before—where others never expected us to be—means that the waters we enter can be pretty rough. Many times it feels as if we're swimming upstream. But every culture and environment has a certain flow. When you learn to find the right "stroke" to go with the flow, without compromising your personal values, your life will be less stressful.

Going with the flow involves asking for divine guidance to show you the people and places and structures that will help you be effective. God always places the people in our paths we are supposed to find. The world calls it coincidence. I call it God's divine plan.

I learned a valuable lesson about going with the flow when I was selected as a White House fellow in 1993. Once I had made it through the intensive interviews in the selection process, I had to go through a final series of placement interviews.

The résumés of all seventeen of the fellows had been sent to the president, the vice president, and all the cabinet secretaries. They in turn had sent the placement office profiles of the candidates they were looking for. Some positions called for a legal background, a financial background, or some other specialty. I was fairly certain that Baptist preacher was not a category that had been profiled.

And I was further dismayed when one of the staffers told me, "Now, if none of your interviews work out, we have a place for you in personnel. Don't worry if you're not a match." *Yeah, right,* I thought as I left the White House fellows office, *I came to Washington so that I could do clerical work for a year.*

That was when I preached myself my grandmother's favorite sermon: "Remember who you are." I thought, *I've made it to this point. I'm going to present myself confidently. I'm not going to try and fake these people out. Just let them see who I am.*

My first interview was in the White House with a woman who worked in the domestic policy office. We chatted for a few minutes, and then I asked her what the domestic policy council did. Instead of answering my question, she had one of her own. "Did you write a book called *Wise Women Bearing Gifts?*"

"Yes, I did."

"I was fascinated with that book," she told me.

The turn in the conversation surprised me. *Well, just go with the flow,* I thought. So I briefly shared with her about being a woman in ministry.

As we were talking, her eyes caught the lapel pin I was wearing. It held a tiny picture of my son, Samuel, who was then nine months old. "Who is that?" she asked, pointing to the pin.

When I told her it was my son, she said, "You know, out of everything you do here in Washington, the most important thing is that you go home at five o'clock and pick that baby up and connect with him. Even if you have to come back to the office late at night or take extra work home, make sure your child sees you every day."

God began to confirm in my spirit that if she were that caring and sensitive about my child, then that was the place for me. I had prayed earnestly about this year in Washington because I knew that it had to work for Samuel and Ron in order for it to be right for me. I had asked God to give me favor and to put me with the right people and places, and he had. The right apartment, the right child care—everything had fallen into place so far. I suddenly knew it would be the same with landing the right position.

Six more interviews had been lined up for me, including one with the late Ron Brown, who was the secretary of commerce. Every interview went well, and when I returned to the White House fellows office, the placement counselor said, "What did you do? How did you pull it off? All seven places offered you jobs."

"I didn't do anything special," I said. "I was just myself."

They thought I must have done something very unusual. But the Holy Spirit had prepared the way for me, and I just went with the flow.

I had been very tempted by the offer from Ron Brown at Commerce and the one from the director of AmeriCorps, the new national volunteer program. But my preference was the job at the White House, working with the domestic policy council. It had not even occurred to me that every single person wanted to be in the White House, and that the competition for that job would be the most fierce. But the Baptist preacher from the Bronx landed the top position.

God's Traffic Signals

Going with the flow is also like learning to drive. To get to our destination safely, without injury to ourselves or others, we have to understand the flow of traffic. We must learn what all the traffic signs and signals mean.

Some of the most vital lessons I've learned have been about understanding, and following, God's direction. While God's general instruction may be to go forward, he sometimes signals us to slow down, to yield, or to stop completely for a period. And when we learn to go with God's traffic flow, we get rid of a lot of the stress in our lives.

Walk/Don't Walk

Ephesians 4:1 tells us to "walk worthy" of our calling. The passage is talking about living in a manner that brings honor to the Lord and fosters unity in the body of Christ. But note that it doesn't say "run worthy." It is not necessary to move at a frenetic pace all of the time. In Christian circles we talk about our "walk" with God, but too many us of approach the Christian life like a 10K run.

Urban metropolises move at a frenzied pace, and most of the people don't know why they are moving so fast. It just seems to come with the territory. My office window overlooks a busy intersection. A lot of traffic passes by that corner—people as well as cars. There are laws against jaywalking, and traffic lights that flash *Walk/Don't Walk*. But many people are in such a hurry that they won't wait for the light to change. And some of them won't go all the way to the intersection; they cross in the middle of a busy street, dodging the traffic.

Sometimes we spiritually jaywalk through life, plunging into the traffic while God is flashing the *Don't Walk* signal. A jaywalker has a legal goal: crossing the street. He just goes about reaching that goal in an illegal, and often dangerous, manner. Similarly we may have a desire or a plan that is in God's will, but we don't wait for his timing. And the results can bring injury and pain.

You will find that most things in life are worth waiting for. And *all* things in Christ are worth the wait. If I had received all of the things I thought I was ready for, I would be a messed-up woman today. There were some jobs that would have probably destroyed me, some relationships that would have crushed me. Even though God's *Don't Walk* lessons can be painful as we're going through them, in retrospect we can see his wisdom.

Before I met my wonderful husband (I'll tell you that story in a later chapter), I went through several bad relationships. One of them was with a man I will call Joe (not his real name).

I met Joe, who pastored a small church in Harlem, in seminary. In a predominantly white school, all the black students get to know each other, so it was inevitable that we would meet. One day I was sitting next to Joe in class when our legs touched underneath the table. The next thing I knew we were talking about meeting after class.

We began dating frequently, and I thought it was marvelous for two ministers to be in love. I didn't know that there was an undercurrent operating behind the scenes. Joe was an officer in the local Baptist ministers' conference, and at that time they weren't ready for women to play a role in ministry. Some of his peers were pressuring Joe to end our relationship. They made it clear that he would be disowned if he married a woman who thought she could be a pastor.

Added to that pressure was my quick rise to "stardom," which eclipsed Joe's career in the church world. He wasn't handling it well, but I didn't see that either.

When I was elected senior pastor of Mariners' Temple, the church held a week of special services. Joe was there for all the services, which culminated in my installation. Some eleven hundred people attended that event, and it was given extensive press coverage. During the service, one of our preaching teachers leaned over to Joe and said, "When are you going to marry Suzan? You two have been a public item for a couple of years."

After the service that night Joe took me out to dinner. I was so excited, I was floating on air. I am bubbly by nature, but that night I was absolutely effervescent. Joe, however, was subdued. And I finally came down from the clouds when he began talking about our future.

"There's just too much pressure," he said. "I'm getting pressure on one side to marry you and pressure on the other side not to."

"You have to marry me because you love me, Joe, not because of pressure." I was deeply in love, and I was convinced that we would inevitably get married. What could be more perfect than two preachers getting married? It was bound to be God's will for us.

"You know I love you, Suzan."

"Well, what then? Are you saying that the time is not right? Or that you definitely won't marry me? Where do you stand?"

Joe became vague and wouldn't give me an answer. All the enthusiasm I had felt earlier was gone. My bubble had burst. What had started out as one of the most glorious days of my life suddenly turned into one of the worst.

I went home in tears. I had reached a professional height and, at the very same moment, a personal low point. I faced the challenge of pouring my heart into my ministry, just when that heart was breaking.

A few days later Joe called from the airport. He was on his way out of the country. In his roundabout way, he told me it was over.

"Joe, how do you invest this much time with someone and then brush it off so lightly with a lousy phone call from the airport?"

"I gotta go. My plane's leaving." Click.

And when the telephone line went dead, so did a three-year relationship with a man who didn't even have the nerve to tell me in person.

In retrospect, long after the reservoir of tears had been emptied and my bruised heart had healed, I could clearly see that the relationship was not right. God had been flashing the *Don't Walk* sign at me, but I was rushing along so fast with my plans for my life that I didn't see it.

Joe was very guarded and never allowed me to spend any time with his family. Although I had taken Joe to meet my family and they included him in family occasions, Joe went to great lengths to keep me away from his. That should have been a warning to me.

I also should have sensed that he was not secure enough to handle my success in the ministry. I should have been aware of the tremendous peer pressure he was under *not* to marry a woman minister. I faced plenty of obstacles in breaking down the barriers, so the signs were all around me. If Joe had truly loved me, then it would have worked in spite of all the opposition. Clearly he didn't have that kind of love in his heart. God knew what was in Joe's heart, and God spared me the tragedy of finding it out on the other side of marriage.

While it was painful at the time, I am very grateful that God did not allow me to marry Joe. Instead of being unequally yoked with someone who could not affirm my gifts and my calling, I am now married to a man who loves me without reservation, who supports my ministry, who undergirds my ministry with prayer, and who is not afraid to tell me to chill out when I need it.

So when God was telling me *Don't Walk*, he was not saying that marriage was not his will for me. He was saying that this man was not the right one, that it was not the right time. I just needed to wait at the intersection until the light changed and the signal said *Walk*.

Slow Traffic Keep Right

Have you ever watched a driver who is in a big hurry? Before the stoplight even changes she is revving up the engine, ready to peel out and get ahead of the traffic flow. She honks the horn as she races away, making sure nobody gets in front of her.

Many people approach life like the driver in a hurry. They do not have the discipline necessary for them to get from one point to the next. They repeat the same lessons in life until they get it right. The driver who speeds because she is in a big hurry often misses the synchronization of the traffic lights, so she ends up having to stop at the next intersection anyway. All her hurrying gained her nothing.

I am very prone to speeding physically and spiritually. I used to rush around so fast that even on vacations I needed three or four days to slow down enough to enjoy myself. I have had to be intentional about finding places and times where I don't move at such a hectic pace.

In November 1996 Dr. Wyatt T. Walker, a leading civil rights figure and a pastor here in New York, invited me to lead a church delegation to South Africa. He had been very close to Nelson Mandela and the antiapartheid movement there. Ours would be one of the first organized visits of a black church to South Africa after apartheid. A group of fourteen from my church joined a group from Dr. Walker's church for the historic trip.

As tour host, I was busy keeping track of my group through action-packed days. On a tour everyone wants to see as much as possible. People don't want to miss anything because they don't know when they'll ever get to come back. (In fact, since many on the tour were senior citizens, they knew it would probably be their one and only trip.)

After several days, my stress level was way over the top. I desperately needed time away from the crowd. I got up very early one morning and went out to enjoy some time alone. My previous explorations of our neighborhood had led me to an oceanfront park area about five blocks from our hotel, so I headed in that direction.

I found a bench and sat with my legs pulled up and my arms wrapped around my knees. Tilting my head back, I inhaled deeply, savoring the fresh air with its saltwater tang. I relished the distance from my busyness as I enjoyed the solitary moments thousands of miles across the Atlantic from the bustle of the Bronx. Away from the pollution-choked air. Away from the crowded, dirty streets. Away from the wailing sirens and the commotion of city life. Here the only sounds were the crashing of the surf and the calling of seagulls.

My eyes surveyed the seascape, trying to memorize the sights, the way the ocean dissolved into the distant horizon, the choreography of the waves. As I watched the whitecaps splashing and spilling over the rocks, I imagined a Spanish dancer swaying and swishing her skirt, a satiny skirt of turquoise tipped with white frothy lace.

The waves danced. And my spirit began to dance as God placed his hand on me. All of that pent-up stress flowed out of me. It was released into the ocean and washed away with the outgoing tide. All too often my most intimate spiritual connection with God takes place in the pulpit when I am preaching. That day God preached to me from his pulpit, the beauty of his creation: "The earth is the LORD's, and the fullness thereof" (Ps. 24:1 KJV).

Reflecting on God's touch at that moment, I understood what David meant in Psalm 23 when he said, "He restoreth my soul" (v.3 KJV). In those few brief minutes with God my soul was restored.

I opted to skip the tour that day in favor of watching the waves dance. It was time to slow down and let those in the fast lane pass me.

Even God took a day off. "And He rested on the seventh day from all His work which He had done" (Gen. 2:2). Is it time you slowed down? Taking time off when you need it is one of the ways of honoring the God who created you. If God rested after creating the entire universe, then why shouldn't you?

If you don't slow down when God prompts you to, he may allow circumstances to come into your life that will force you to yield the right of way. That's a lesson I learned the hard way, and I share this painful episode with you now in the hopes that you will learn from my mistake and be spared from a similar pain.

Yield Right of Way

As I began a new ministry in the Bronx, I intended to do things differently and not make the same mistakes I had in the past. I thought that I had arrived at a point of maturity where I would not overload myself and not tolerate things that were unhealthy for me. However, even with all the stress I had eliminated, the pace of my life began to pick up again.

My old neighborhood welcomed me back and embraced me in such a way that my ego got involved. People started asking me to serve on different community boards, and before long I was falling into that old trap of trying to be all things to all people. I was also traveling and speaking quite a bit, and I was moving so fast that my head did not listen to my body when it started telling me to slow down.

In June 1997 I flew to Virginia for the Hampton Ministers' Conference. As an officer of the conference, I sat on the stage with the other speakers and presenters. Many of the messages that week were about birth and life, a theme that captured my attention because I was enjoying a season of new birth in my ministry. During one of the Wednesday sessions, a friend leaned over to whisper something to me. I started to answer and then paused in midsentence, as something the speaker was saying registered in my mind.

"You're not pregnant, are you?" my friend asked.

The question startled me. I had been feeling sick ever since I arrived, but I thought it was just a little sluggishness. *All I need is a week at Hampton*, I had told myself. *That will cure me.*

But enthusiasm for the conference had not charged my batteries enough to pull me out of my doldrums. I began to think of what my friend said. Could I really be pregnant? *Well, there's an easy way to find out*, I thought. The next day, Thursday, I went to the drugstore and bought a home pregnancy test. Back in my hotel room I took the test and watched the little strip of paper change colors, telling me that I was, indeed, pregnant.

My body had been trying to tell me the news, but I had been moving so fast that I could not read the signs. I had been a mother twice already; I knew what it felt like to be pregnant. This time I had fooled myself into believing I was just tired and run down.

For a moment all I could think was, *This is a very, very full year, and I've got so much to do. It's not a great time to be pregnant.* Yet, deep down, an excitement was stirring. I did want to have a third child.

With mixed emotions, I began to pray and thank God for the gift of new life developing inside me. "I accept this pregnancy, Lord, and I recognize that everything else in my life will have to take a backseat for now."

Almost as soon as I prayed that prayer, I began seeing signs that I might be losing the baby. On Friday morning I called my doctor in New York and told her what was happening. "Stop everything you're doing," she said. "And as soon as you get back here, I want to see you in my office."

On Saturday I flew home. I was tired physically, but spiritually refreshed. I was a little worried about my pregnancy, but I didn't think it wasn't an emergency. Besides, it was a weekend. My doctor wouldn't be in the office. *I'm not that sick,* I told myself. *I'll see the doctor first thing Monday. Everything will be okay.*

But everything was not okay. I preached three times on Sunday, and by the end of the Sunday evening service I knew that my condition was serious. I went home and crawled into bed, my emotions numb. I had learned I was pregnant on Thursday. I had struggled with the news but accepted it as a gift from God. Surely I could not be losing this baby just three days later.

Early Monday morning I went to the doctor. She examined me, confirmed that I had miscarried, and gave my body the necessary medical attention. Then she stepped outside the room to give me some privacy.

I lay on the table for about half an hour, lost in a horrible, crushing loneliness. My womb was empty and so, for the moment, was my soul. I had lost close relatives before—my father and my favorite aunt—but the one I had lost this time had been living inside me. There was nothing in my experience to which I could compare it.

Finally I began to pray silently. *Lord, where is the blessing in all this? There's always a blessing. Help me to see it.* In that moment of great emotional pain, I began to think of other women who had lain on an operating table just like this, crushed by the same overwhelming sense of loss: Another woman, without two healthy sons at home, who lay on the table after losing the child she had always longed for. A scared young woman, all alone, who lay on the table after an abortion, weighing the enormity of her decision and desperately wishing her family had known what was happening to her.

God showed me that because of my pain I would be more sensitive to people who had experienced considerable losses. It would bring a depth to my ministry, a profound compassion that comes only from profound suffering.

But even with that word from God, I did not learn the one lesson that should have been the most obvious to me. When I finally pulled myself together, I got dressed and went into the doctor's office. "You need to rest for forty-eight hours," she said. "You're going to do that, aren't you?" She looked at me intently because she knew the frantic pace of my lifestyle.

"Yes," I said. Even while I said it, I knew I was not going to stop. I was already making a mental checklist of all the things I needed to be doing. *There are just a few things I have to do in the office first*, I told myself. *Then I'll get some rest.*

When I got home from the doctor's office, I called my friend Nina. I've known Nina since the seventh grade. We've always been so close that we tell people we're cousins. "I need to tell you what happened today," I said, my voice breaking. As I shared the news of my miscarriage with her, Nina sympathized with me and comforted me as only a close sister-friend or cousin can do.

I finally said, "Well, I'd better be going. I need to get to the office and do a few things."

Nina went ballistic. "Whoa! Wait a minute," she said. "Didn't the doctor tell you to get some rest?" My sister-friend would not listen to my attempt to protest. Instead, she put up a yield sign.

"We're talking about your health, Suzan. What kind of message does it send the people around you when you don't take care of yourself? What would you tell one of your church members who was in the same situation?"

I started crying as I thought about what Nina said. I would *never* counsel someone to do what I was doing. Of course, I would tell her to follow the doctor's orders and take the necessary time to rest and heal. I would say that her health was too important to jeopardize. Why, then, would I put my health in jeopardy and not allow myself to take time off? Did I think I was not significant enough to merit the same concern I would show for one of my church members?

Brought back to my senses by this dear friend who confronted me, I went to bed. I yielded my agenda. I took a few days off. For the first time in ages, I puttered around the house, taking care of some things that needed my attention, and that included taking care of myself. And you know what? The office survived without me. We probably got more accomplished in the days following my return because I was fully rested.

Because of the strain on my body, I had been unable to maintain my pregnancy until the time for a normal delivery. That's what a miscarriage is, the inability to carry to full term. The Lord showed me that there can be miscarriages in the spiritual realm as well as the physical realm. You may be pregnant with possibilities the Creator has placed inside of you. Be careful. You want to be able to carry them to full term. Take the time you need. Take the time you deserve for yourself. Yield your agenda to God's. Let him have the right of way.

Day by Day

Day by day and with each passing moment,
Strength I find to meet my trials here;
Trusting in my Father's wise bestowment,
I've no cause for worry or for fear.
He whose heart is kind beyond all measure
Gives unto each day what He deems best—
Lovingly, its part of pain and pleasure,
Mingling toil with peace and rest.

Revival fires that swept the United States and Europe in the mid-nineteenth century gave birth to the gospel music publishing industry. Some of the most prominent hymn writers were women: Fanny Crosby in the United States, Frances Ridley Havergal in England, and Lina Sandell Berg in Sweden, author of "Day by Day."

When Lina was twelve, God healed her of a paralysis that had kept her bedridden for several years. When Lina was twenty-six, she was traveling by ship with her father, a Lutheran pastor. As she watched helplessly, he fell overboard and drowned. Without doubt, Lina had known her "part of pain and pleasure." But she never lost her childlike faith and trust in God, which found beautiful expression in the 650 hymns she penned.

Stop, Look, and Listen

As we have seen, going with the flow means getting into God's traffic flow. He places signals in our lives, telling us when to walk and when not to, when to slow down, and when to yield. But sometimes God tells us to stop completely.

behind them and the Red Sea in front of them, there was no way to go forward. The solution was not to jump in the water and start swimming. The solution was found in stopping and letting God work out the situation supernaturally.

> And Moses said to the people, "Do not be afraid. Stand still, and see the salvation of the LORD, which He will accomplish for you today. For the Egyptians whom you see today, you shall see again no more forever. The LORD will fight for you, and you shall hold your peace." (Ex. 14:13–14)

It was in the standing still that Moses was given divine direction and the people experienced a miracle that led to their liberation. The Red Sea opened up for them, and they were able to walk across, unhindered, on dry land. But they couldn't go forward until they had stood still and listened to God.

Many people are looking for God in the spectacular, while God is speaking in the stillness. We have to stop long enough to hear God and find out specifically what God would have us to do. He will make a way where there seems to be no way, but we have to be still and quiet while he does it.

Psalm 46:10 notes, "Be still, and know that I am God." God speaks in the quietness. Silence allows us to hear the whispers of God.

Too often we approach prayer in a one-sided fashion: we talk and God listens. But prayer is two-way communication. At some point we have to listen while God talks. That can't happen if we're speaking so much that God can't get a word in edgewise. Does God get a busy signal every time he calls your number? Quit babbling! Be still, and know that he is God.

Be Still, My Soul

Be still, my soul: the Lord is on thy side;
Bear patiently the cross of grief or pain;

Leave to thy God to order and provide;
In every change He faithful will remain.
Be still, my soul: thy best, thy heavenly Friend
Through thorny ways leads to a joyful end.

Be still, my soul: thy God doth undertake
To guide the future as He has the past.
Thy hope, thy confidence let nothing shake;
All now mysterious shall be bright at last.
Be still, my soul: the waves and winds still know
His voice who ruled them while He dwelt below.

Katharina von Schlegel, head of an evangelical women's seminary, wrote this hymn during a time of revival in Germany. It was published around 1752. About a hundred years later, Jane Borthwick translated the hymn into English. The tune, "Finlandia," is from Jean Sibelius's symphonic work celebrating the beauty of his native Finland. It doesn't matter what country or culture or century you're born into—God is the same yesterday, today, and forever. Allow your soul to be still as you reflect on God's unchanging love for you and his provision for your needs.

The world is moving faster than any of us ever imagined. Technology and science have made such inroads that we sometimes feel life is rushing rapidly past us. As life becomes more high-tech and impersonal, we need more than ever to be still and know God. You won't find God's home page on the Internet. His address is not http://www.GOD.com. God is a personal God. He knows you by name. Get in your prayer closet and make the divine connection with him.

When I met my husband, one of the things that attracted me to him was that he would not even ask me on a date until we had both prayed about it. There was an instant chemistry between us, and the sparks were flying. But Ron said, "Let's pray about it first." He knew that I wanted a husband, and he was looking for a wife. We were both seeking a serious relationship. There was no sense in even dating if we didn't have a green light from God.

Praise God for a man who understood that we needed to "stand still" and get direction from God. We heeded God's stop sign. We prayed for several days, and both of us received confirmation that it was okay to proceed with the relationship. Ron and I were willing to wait on God rather than rush into things. As a result, we flow together beautifully now.

Learning to go with the flow requires a road map; our map is God's Word. We also need to tune in God's traffic report; we do that through prayer. That's how we receive God's signals: *Walk/Don't Walk*, *Slow*, *Yield*, or *Stop*.

When you learn to go with the flow, you will truly begin to experience the abundant life Christ came to give us. Are you living life to the fullest? That's the next question we will examine.

CHAPTER EIGHT

Live Abundantly

As a child, I learned that many people live abundantly even in poverty. During all those trips to the South, I recognized that my family in the Bronx was a lot better off financially than some of my relatives. But because everyone shared so generously, there was always an overflow of everything.

Aunt Pet was determined that the poor children she gathered to her mission house in Concord, North Carolina, would know the same abundance. She negotiated with the grocery store and local merchants for discounted, or donated, food and supplies. When she put on a vacation Bible school, she not only fed us spiritually but also threw a feast—not just cookies and Kool-Aid, mind you, but hamburgers, hot dogs, and the trimmings. We had more than the rich kids.

One of the fundamental lessons I learned from my parents is to be grateful for what you have, and whatever you have, share it. They didn't preach this lesson to me; I learned it as a lifestyle.

My mother was a schoolteacher at P.S. 194 in Harlem for twenty-three years. Even though many of the people there were economically disadvantaged, they didn't act poor. There was no poverty of spirit. My family certainly wasn't rich, but we had more than many of our friends. Every weekend my parents brought children from our old neighborhood into our home for a visit. One particular family had eleven children, and when things were just too much to handle in their household, some of the kids would stay with us for a while.

Whenever we went on a trip, my parents would ask, "Who can we take with us this time?" And we were forever thinking up reasons to have a party. Mom would invite the Rendall Presbyterian crowd or the Union Baptist crowd or the people she taught with at P.S. 194. Friends were in our house all the time.

That love for socializing with friends and family is still a part of my life. Sometimes when my kids want to do something special, we'll spread a blanket on the floor and have an indoor picnic. I'll fix spaghetti, or we'll order pizza, and I'll ask the kids, "Do you want to call some friends and invite them to share our picnic?"

More Abundantly

Jesus said, "I have come that they may have life, and that they may have it more abundantly" (John 10:10). With all the emphasis on material goods in our society, we sometimes forget that true abundance includes spiritual and moral values.

Before we can have the abundant life Jesus promised, of course, we must have a relationship with Jesus. We must learn to identify with Christ in everything we do. Many people focus their lives on wearing a certain designer label.

As I left an engagement one evening, I went to retrieve my jacket, and I noticed that mine was very similar to another woman's. Just to make conversation I said, "Our leather jackets are very much alike."

"Oh no," she said, "*mine* is a Donna Karan." It was so important to her to be identified with a popular designer. I wish Christians would be as eager to identify with our Maker and Designer. We should be wearing the Christian label; something should clearly identify us as belonging to Christ.

Through Christ, you and the Father are one. If you are feeling apart from the Father, then it is time to take the necessary steps to renew your relationship with your Maker and Designer. Perhaps an afternoon of prayer or a spiritual retreat is in order, but most important is an attitudinal change that puts Jesus at the center of your life.

Suggestions for a Day of Drawing Near to God

- Thank God for allowing you to see that you need to spend more time with him. Ask him to help you make available the necessary time.
- Go to your calendar. Select at least three dates as possibilities.
- Think about a place where you can have at least five hours without interruptions.
- Inform people who need to know that you are taking a day off. Let your employer know when you plan to be out, and make sure that your responsibilities will be covered in your absence. Let your family know that you will be away on important business, and either have things prepared for them before you leave or allow them the opportunity to do things themselves. For example, you might say, "Dinner will be on your own next Thursday. I have an important commitment."
- It is *not* necessary to tell people what you are doing. This is *your* time with God.
- Make arrangements with the place you're going well in advance. Perhaps you have a vacation home or know of a retreat center. You could go to a local hotel. You do not

have to spend a lot of money. You just need some space. Local denominational offices may be able to suggest places they use for retreats, or they may have their own facilities.

- *Go.*
- Things to take with you include a Bible; a hymnal or list of your favorite worship and devotional songs; a pad and pen; a box lunch or picnic basket.
- Start by reading these Scriptures on prayer: Psalm 61:1–4; Jeremiah 33:3; John 14:13–17; 15:7; Philippians 4:6–7; Hebrews 4:16; 1 John 5:14–15.
- For as long as you are able, pray. End by saying, "Father, I thank you for this time alone with you. Already wonderful things have begun to happen for me just by being here. I want to hear your voice. I want to know you. I love you, Lord. May we have a blessed day together."
- Sing some of your favorite songs aloud. Or put on a worship tape and sing along.
- Make a list of the pressing things in your life that you need help with.
- Ask God for help in dealing with these issues. One by one, call out each name or circumstance on your paper. After each one say, "Hear my prayer, O Lord."
- At the completion of your list, sing a song of victory and celebration, believing in advance that God has heard and already answered.
- Now place yourself before God in a kneeling posture (if you are able). Hold your hands up, with your palms facing toward heaven. This posture says to God, "I am open to receive whatever it is you want to place in my hands."
- Spend the next few moments in complete silence. Try to listen to God.
- Begin to thank God for his movement in your life.
- Take a break. Have lunch. Afterward, begin again with songs.
- Thank God for your time together in the morning and for the food that his hands provided. If you have a hymnal, sing "Great Is Thy Faithfulness."

- Pray specifically for the next part of your journey with God and for spiritual maturity. Ask God to allow you to walk closer with him, to be able to feel his presence even at work, at school, or at home.
- Sing songs of thanksgiving. Close with Psalms 100 and 150.
- Just be still. Write down how you felt this day and anything that God revealed to you. After this day, continue to keep a prayer journal and note answers to prayer.

As I understand abundant life in Christ, it means that I can have all of what God wants me to have. I can live life to the fullest. Living abundantly means finding God's purpose for my life and letting him put a dream in my heart, then pursuing that dream. It means living *my* life to the fullest, not someone else's.

Have you been trying to keep up with the Joneses for so long that you've forgotten what *you* desire in life? For example, some people don't enjoy big houses, but because that has been so ingrained in our society as an ideal measure of abundant living, they sacrifice a whole lot of fun to have that dream house—when it's not even their dream.

Some women are not ready for marriage or children, but the pressure on them is relentless. Parents, aunts and uncles, and even friends ask, "When are you getting married?" And as soon as they marry, the question changes to, "When are we going to see some grandkids?" For some, it may not be the right time or the right choice. And what happens if a woman is unable to have children?

How many have lived their lives under stress induced by others who are unkind and insensitive meddlers? Countless people live someone else's dream, or try to, but never match up. Their resentment builds and builds for years, and for them, life is empty rather than full.

The joy of living in this time in history, especially for women in the workforce, is that we do not have to stay anywhere we do not like. As long as you have evaluated where you are financially and factored in things such as benefits for you and your family (if you have one), then you can have four or five careers in a lifetime.

The bottom line is that you do not have to satisfy anyone other than yourself and your God. When you completely identify with Christ, when you draw your purpose and meaning in life from him, you will be able to pursue your dream with confidence. And you will enjoy abundant living no matter what your circumstances.

Have Some Fun

Another aspect of abundant living that we sometimes ignore is having fun. Yes, Christians can have fun!

Somewhere along the way we have become mentally trapped into a rigidity that invites stress and more stress into our lives. All work and no play makes Jack a dull boy; it makes Jacqueline a doubly dull woman. We must allow time for recreation or re-creation, allowing God to replenish what has been depleted. We need to take time away from the ordinary to do things that bring unrestricted joy and fun.

Some Christians cringe at the thought of socializing. But the Bible shows Christ on many occasions at a social gathering or party. In a very real sense he was—and is—the Life of the party. *Can I get a witness?*

If we have new life in Christ, then we should be celebrating that life. Every time we get together should be a time of joy and fellowship. We need frequent times of communion and fellowship with Christ, and we need fellowship with our brothers and sisters in Christ—and it does not always have to be in a church environment.

One of the most profound bonding experiences for our congregation was not in a worship setting at all. Last summer we went on a boat ride around New York Harbor. We sailed out under the stars and viewed the spectacular lights of the city. We played music from the sixties and seventies and sang along with the oldies. The kids got a kick out of seeing some of the adults show off the dances popular when they were teenagers. Many of the people had been conditioned to think that Christians couldn't get together just to have fun, but we broke out of that restrictive mind-set. That night we laughed and enjoyed being with one another.

Recently our congregation went bowling after church one Sunday. We had so much fun, and I had the opportunity to relate to the people, especially the young ones, in an informal way. Seeing their pastor at the bowling alley, not just in the pulpit, forged a new bond. Through experiences like these, we draw closer as friends and as fellow Christians.

Planning to Have Fun

What is something you really enjoy doing, something you haven't done in a long time that would bring a smile to your face? Make a list of those things and some friends who would enjoy doing them with you.

Now look at your calendar. Find a day this week that you can do one of the things you have just listed, either alone or with a friend. Then do it. And if you have fun doing it, then write in a time when you can do it again, or go to the next item on your list and schedule a time for it.

Remember that fun does not have to cost you. But if it does, you deserve it. *Fund your fun.*

Learn to see God in everything. Yes, God is very present in worship services and prayer gatherings at the church, but God is also in the laughter of your children at the circus and in the smile on the face of a senior citizen you've thrown a birthday party for. A wonderful old song expresses this thought that God is present in smiles and laughter: "For God has smiled on me; he has set me free. God has smiled on me; he's been good to me."

In a book I edited for women, *Sister to Sister*,[1] Joann Stevens wrote a meditation entitled "A Sisterly Celebration," describing an occasion when women gathered at the home of a friend for the sole purpose of having fun. No agenda. No business meeting. No church conference. Just pure fun. How healing the testimonies were of the sisters whose lives were touched! A woman who had just had a baby was blessed by a few hours without the responsibilities of caring for a newborn. She was also able to overcome the guilt she felt at leaving her child with someone else for the first time. Another woman, who had just moved to town, felt welcomed and accepted. She made new friends, learned where the post office was, and found a hairstylist. And the birthday girl who threw the bash felt restored just by the presence of her friends.

Fun does not have to cost anything, yet it is priceless. One of the richest sources of fun in your life can be your friends.

Find a Friend

I have several close friends who have been with me through all kinds of weather. They are the ones who allow me to be the "real me." We laugh together and cry together. We help each other through the storms of life and celebrate the joys. We look out for each other. When someone needs a job reference, one of us is happy to give it. When one friend's children or family come to the city to attend college, we make sure they're okay and know they have someone to call when they need something.

Nina, whom I've already mentioned, has been my friend and family since prep school. Our parents helped form the Black Students Parents' Association at our predominantly white school. We started college together and looked like Mutt and Jeff as we went everywhere on campus. Nina is very petite and tiny, perhaps five feet two inches, while I'm built for sports and stand nearly six feet tall. We may be physical opposites, but we're spiritual sisters. We have truly been through thick and thin, and we still speak to each other at least once a week.

Blest Be the Tie that Binds

Blest be the tie that binds
Our hearts in Christian love;
The fellowship of kindred minds
Is like to that above.

As a teenager, John Fawcett came to Christ and was called to the ministry while the great British evangelist George White-field was preaching in an open field. About ten years later, in 1765, the Lord gave Fawcett a flock to pastor, a tiny Baptist church in the very poor village of Wainsgate. His salary was a paltry twenty-five pounds a year, part of it paid in wool and potatoes.

The young Fawcett family grew—four children in five years—and the family was close to starvation, living on porridge and potatoes. When a large church in London called him as pastor, Fawcett accepted. It would mean an adequate salary and greater opportunities for ministry.

The Fawcetts sold their furniture, packed their belongings, and prepared to leave. Fawcett preached a farewell sermon to his Wainsgate flock. As the parishioners brought a cart around to load the family's few belongings and say goodbye, everyone began to weep. And John and Mary realized they could not leave their friends, no matter how great the enticement.

The next Sunday "Fawcett preached from Luke 12:15, 'A man's life consisteth not in the abundance of the things he possesseth,' and after the sermon he lined out, and the congregation sang the hymn he had written the previous midnight: *Blest Be the Tie that Binds*."[2]

Fawcett remained in Wainsgate for fifty-four years, and the Lord richly blessed his ministry. He established a seminary, built a new church, published a volume of hymns, and wrote several books, one of which became a favorite of King George III.

Another friend, Carol, and I met at college, and we discovered our parents had known each other in the 1950s. Two weeks after Carol was in my wedding, I was in hers. We are godmothers to each other's children. Although she works just two blocks from my church, circumstances don't allow us to get together as much as we would like. But each of us knows the other is just a phone call away.

I could mention several other close friends who mean the world to me. Some of them I may get to see only once a year because we are all women on the move. But we write, call, or visit as often as possible.

Sometimes our visits are extremely short. I recently visited with one of my dear friends for two hours. Yolanda King, "Yoki," who is Martin Luther King's oldest child, has been a good friend since we went to Africa together shortly after college. Yoki called to let me know she would be flying into New York for the funeral of Betty Shabazz, Malcolm X's widow. Unfortunately I would be heading out of town shortly after her arrival. But we made it a point to connect, and we treasured those two hours of nonstop talking and laughter. That visit brought me such joy.

Take time to enjoy your friends. Allow yourself to have fun. Learn to live abundantly no matter how meager your resources. And learn to live victoriously whatever your circumstances. That's the next word of wisdom for the woman who wants to be too blessed to be stressed.

CHAPTER NINE

Live
Victoriously

Hampton, Virginia, is the black preachers' mecca. For an entire year, we talk about going to the Hampton Ministers' Conference, and once it's over, we talk about it until it rolls around the next year. It's the one don't-miss event in our ministry circles.

I went to Hampton for the first time in 1982, just after I was ordained. Some of my seminary buddies invited me to make the trek with them, and on the long drive down to Virginia we encountered many other ministers heading to the conference. They would tell us what an exciting experience we were in for and how we were going to hear the giants of the faith, the "hall of fame" of our denomination. "Absolutely the best preaching in the nation," they said.

When you were invited to speak at Hampton, you knew you had arrived. Even to read the Scripture prior to the evening's speaker was an honor. And in all the preceding years, no woman had ever been invited to participate. Hampton was an all-boys' world.

My first conference was the year a woman, the Reverend Dr. Ella Mitchell, finally stepped onto the dais at Hampton to read the Holy Scripture. Along with her husband, this stately senior woman had paved the way for a new wave of women. "I wonder how many Hamptons she had to sit out before this happened?" I asked one of my friends. She didn't know either, but we knew we were witnessing history.

Having arrived two hours early to get choice seats, we sat in the front row of the balcony. It was hot in Ogden Hall, literally and spiritually. An ordinary college auditorium was transformed into an anointed sanctuary. The singing was phenomenal, the sermons awesome, the excitement electrifying. From our perch we watched the "who's who" of the preaching world ascend the podium. "Who's that?" I would ask. "Where is he from?" Afterward, we waited at the side door, hoping we would get an opportunity to introduce ourselves or to be introduced.

By my third trip to Hampton, I was making history myself. I had been elected senior pastor of Mariners' Temple and had turned around a dying church. We were sitting in Ogden Hall one night that year when the lights went out. All 2,500 of us kept right on singing.

As the hymn ended, I suddenly heard a voice—unamplified, since we had lost the electricity—yelling, "Is Sujay Johnson in the room? Can she make her way to the stage?"

Oh, my. What have I done? was my first thought. But I slowly made my way to the stage in the darkened auditorium.

"Would you read the Scripture for us, Reverend Johnson?"

I was so nervous, my fingers wouldn't work. Someone else flipped open my Bible for me and found the text. I had been reading the Scripture before the sermon at my home church for years, and I had even been preaching for years, but this was different. Now I represented all the women who had never even had a shot at participating in Hampton.

Finally the lights came back on, and I was on stage at Hampton, and I was *on*. I read the Bible as I've never read it before. If that had been an Olympic competition for Scripture reading, I would have taken top honors—bronze and silver didn't cross my mind; I was going for the gold.

When I took a seat on the platform, I was shaking, and I shook through most of the sermon. *I'm on the stage at Hampton. It can't get any better than this,* I thought.

After the service, I exited through the same door as the hall of famers. I was feeling good about God and about myself. I felt included, like one of the "old boys." So I enthusiastically reached over to shake the hand of one of the old-timers everyone admired. "I'm Sujay Johnson," I said.

"I know who you are," he said as he pushed my hand away roughly. People were standing all around, and I wished the earth would just open up and swallow me at that moment.

Some of the older vanguard of the organization were firmly against women in ministry, and their vocal opposition came as something of a surprise to me. In the environment in which I grew up, men and women were not restricted to narrowly defined roles. In our household there was no notion that women do the cooking and men take out the garbage—men and women did both jobs, and any other job that needed to be done. I was taught to aim for whatever I wanted to be, not what society said I had to be. Although I had experienced plenty of racism before, the church world was the first place I experienced sexism.

When women began entering the ministry, some men felt we had invaded their turf. We were not trying to take anything away from anyone, however; we wanted to receive only what God had for us. And we had to be obedient to his call to preach whether or not anybody else recognized that call.

So the next year I went back to Hampton, and the year after that, and every year since then. I wouldn't miss it for the world. I never got angry or resentful at anyone who did not accept me as a woman in ministry. I continued to extend my hand, introduce myself, and even hug anyone who would let me. I laughed and joked around with the other ministers, and I even played tennis and basketball with them. I wanted them to see that we could be friends. I was not going to go away, so they would have to learn how to deal with me, just as I had to learn how to deal with them.

A New Era Begins

Time certainly changes things. Some seven years after I first read the Scripture at Hampton, I was invited to speak at the Women in Ministry Hour. Just the receipt of the invitation letter sent chills up my spine. For eleven months I wrestled with my message. Then the moment finally arrived. Ogden Hall was again filled to capacity. My stomach was filled with butterflies.

In previous years when a woman stood to speak, hundreds of men got up and left. I had been praying that the men would stay that year. I didn't know if what I had to say was so powerful, but I just didn't want to deal with that awful feeling of rejection.

As I was introduced, I heard movement. The lights in the audience were dark, so I couldn't see all that was happening. I could see shadows moving, so I thought the men were leaving. Then I began to hear voices approaching the stage. "We're with you, Sujay. Make us proud." People weren't leaving: they were trying to get close to the stage to cheer me on!

When I finished my message, hundreds were on their feet applauding and shouting. God had taken control of the situation, and a new era at Hampton had begun. From that point on, women would be invited to preach.

In 1996 I was honored to be nominated as the first female officer in the eighty-year history of Hampton. Some of the men who had originally been opposed to women in ministry later told me how proud they were of me. I have just completed my first tenure as an officer of Hampton, and I must say that the male officers have treated me with dignity and respect as a friend and colleague.

In fact, many of my fellow ministers have become friends and mentors and are very supportive of my ministry. They have come to realize that I never wanted to be anything but God's servant. Now we all join hand in hand and go forward for the kingdom of God.

One thing I've learned is that you can't go forward to victory if you remain stuck in the past. *Hello, somebody!*

Let Go of the Past

For many people, things that were done to them in the past or things they have done to themselves have caused an inner paralysis. They have held on to their anger, resentment, and embarrassment for so long, they cannot escape their emotional prisons. It's as if they have built up a wall around themselves so that nothing good can come in and nothing good will get out.

In the book of Philippians the apostle Paul declared, "Forgetting those things which are behind and reaching forward to those things which are ahead, I press toward the goal for the prize of the upward call of God in Christ Jesus" (3:13–14). Pressing toward the mark requires intentional action. It takes effort to move beyond the past, sometimes a *lot* of effort.

Although we can't change the past, we don't have to stay stuck in it. Some people may need professional help to allow them to break free from past hurts or even abuse. For others, letting go of the past just means growing up. That doesn't mean it's easy. If resentment has left a bitter taste in your mouth for a long, long time, then you may need additional support. There are wonderful Christian counselors and ministers these days who understand the kind of spiritual help you need. If you need help, get it—before the bitterness and resentment you are harboring manifest themselves in loss of appetite, hair loss, ulcers, or other illnesses.

Get a New Vision

To let go of the past and learn to live victoriously, we need a new vision. We need to have our eyes opened.

In Scripture, the prophet Isaiah described an eye-opening experience. "In the year that King Uzziah died," he wrote, "I saw the Lord sitting on a throne, high and lifted up, and the train of His robe filled the temple" (6:1). Isaiah remembered it well because it was in the year that someone he had placed in a high priority died. Sometimes we place folks on a pedestal, even above God. And God sometimes has to remove them so that we can see him again.

When Isaiah saw God, he said, "Woe is me, for I am undone! / Because I am a man of unclean lips" (6:5). God sent an angel to clean up his mouth. Sometimes we say things God is not pleased with. Some of us say the s word, and I don't mean Savior. And so God sometimes has to clean up our conversation before he can use us.

But in every worship experience, God is not only cleaning out our mouths, he is also sending an angel to perform spiritual cataract surgery—because some of us have coverings over our eyes. We thought we saw Christ, but we've not seen him the way we need to.

If you want to live victoriously, you must begin to see things differently. Your gaze should first turn inward. Stop looking at everybody else's faults, and start saying, "Lord, change me." Stop talking about the "speck of sawdust" in someone else's eye, and look at the whole "plank" that's in yours (Matt. 7:3 NIV). The first step to getting a new vision is to look inside yourself and confront your own stuff. Your "stuff" could be something in the past that you haven't gotten over, or it could be an attitude that blames everybody else for your problems. *Am I stepping on any toes?*

The second step to getting a new vision is to allow your gaze to go upward. The psalmist wrote,

> I will lift up my eyes to the hills—
> From whence comes my help?
> My help comes from the LORD. (Ps. 121:1–2)

Your help does not come from your congressional representative or any other public official. Your help comes from the Lord.

In the United States we are blessed with the best form of government on earth. Government is good. But the government is not your Provider. Your employer is not your Provider. Jehovah Jireh is your Provider. He is the one on whom you can rely. So begin to look upward—lift up your eyes. *Hello, somebody!*

Every time God wants to use someone, he changes that person's vision—as he did with Paul on the road to Damascus or John on the island of Patmos. And the Lord will begin to change your vision when you're ready to let him do a work in you.

My husband and I have a wonderful corner apartment. We have lots of windows that let the light in, and I love the view. I didn't realize that I needed a change of vision, however, until something wonderful happened last summer: a work crew washed my windows. All of a sudden I could see with new clarity, and colors became more vibrant. When you invite Jesus into your life, it's like having your windows washed. He washes away all the film that's built up over the years.

Open My Eyes, That I May See

Open my eyes, that I may see
Glimpses of truth Thou hast for me;
Place in my hands the wonderful key
That shall unclasp and set me free;
Silently now I wait for Thee,
Ready, my God, Thy will to see;

> Open my eyes, illumine me,
> Spirit divine!

Clara Scott, a music teacher in the Ladies' Seminary of Lyons, Iowa, wrote the words and music for this hymn in 1895. It is one of my favorites because it shows all our senses involved in apprehending and obeying God's will. The second verse says, "Open my ears, that I may hear." The third verse asks God to "open my mouth," that I may speak the truth, and "open my heart," that I may share his love.

Receive a New Vitality

When you get a new vision, you should receive new vitality. Something should happen on Sunday when you come to worship. It should be different from Monday through Saturday. Like the psalmist, you should be saying, "I was glad when they said to me, / 'Let us go into the house of the Lord'" (122:1).

But many folks come to church and appear to be dead. It reminds me of the television show *ER*. There's always a scene where an ambulance brings in a patient on a stretcher. Everybody is running and yelling complicated instructions that the average viewer can't comprehend. The background music is building—*ba dum ba dum ba dum ba dum ba DUM*.

And you know what's coming next. One of the doctors grabs the paddles and yells, "Clear!" He slams the paddles on the patient's chest, pumping an electrical charge into the body. Nothing happens. So the doctor tells the nurse to increase the charge, and then he jolts the patient again. Nothing. They go through the routine a third time, and finally the patient's body jumps up and you hear the heart monitor start beeping. The body appeared to be dead, but there was still enough life to resuscitate.

That's what worship is like. Many folks come to church as lifeless as that patient in the emergency room. The choir might as well

be singing *ba dum ba dum ba dum ba dum ba DUM.* The congregation sings and shouts and praises, and God pumps the hearts of
those Christians who were dead on arrival. Nothing. They just sit
there, still in cardiac arrest. The elders read Scripture and lead the
people in prayer, and God pumps their hearts again. Nothing.
Finally God says, "Here's my anointed preacher. Now come alive!"

And I know there's enough power to resuscitate the lifeless
because all that divine electricity is flowing through me. When
I preach, I'm applying Holy Spirit paddles on hearts, and I expect
to see some bodies jump up and to hear some signs of life.

You've got enough life in you to resuscitate. God blew his
breath into you. When you come to church, you should have
something to say. You should have a song to sing. Receive the
vitality of God when you come to worship.

Give Expression to Victory

When the Lord changes your vision and you receive new
vitality, then walk and talk in victory. Every Christian should
walk like a victor. You shouldn't think of yourself more highly
than you ought to, but you should know you're somebody. At
my church we say, "Don't be stuck up; be prayed up." Walk with
the victory. Talk with the victory. Hold your head up high.

I saw an unforgettable expression of victory on a trip to South
Africa as a White House fellow. We went to a meeting in a large
auditorium. A choir of sisters in their beautiful African dress
began to sing in one of the local dialects. As the sisters started
singing, their bodies started moving gracefully. They were doing
the *toyi toyi.*

Then Bishop Desmond Tutu got up, and the music got to him
too. Church folks in America get hung up about dancing, but
Africans dance every chance they get. So the bishop said, "Don't
leave me out!" And he started swaying with the choir. Then the
president, Nelson Mandela, came to the podium. He was standing there so straight and dignified, trying to be cool. But the

music got to him too. And before long he was doing the *toyi toyi*.

Why were they dancing? The *toyi toyi* is a victory dance. Their bodies were expressing what their souls wanted to say. When Nelson Mandela joined in the *toyi toyi*, his body and spirit were saying, "Once I was a prisoner, but now I'm the president. Look what God has done."

Sometimes you can't put your victory into words. You just know that God is so good, you can't sit still. You can't be cool. Your body has to move. Every time we get to church, we should do a victory dance. I can't keep my joy to myself. I've got to shout. I've got to dance the victory. Some people may not like it, but I can't help that. They didn't give me this joy, and they can't take it away. *Can I get a witness?*

Sing in the Midnight Hour

Earlier I shared with you how I started a new church in the Bronx and how wonderful this springtime in my ministry has been. While it has been a season of new birth and growth, there have also been some dark "midnight" hours.

Our church is located on one of the busiest corners in the community—the kind of location that churches and businesses dream about. People cannot miss seeing the church as they walk or drive by or wait at the bus stop directly in front. But our beginning there was rough. The first winter we were in the building, we had no heat. During those bitterly cold months, the Lord kept me from getting sick, even though my office was a deep freeze.

As I was praying about the situation, God led me to Acts 16 and the story of Paul and Silas in prison at Philippi. God showed me that the situation we were going through was one of the "midnights" of our ministry. Midnights always occur when we are on a roll. People tend to mess with us when we are doing well. We have an expression for it: "When God gets to blessin', the devil gets to messin'."

Paul and Silas had been on a spiritual roll. Their ministry had been blessed, and people were being healed and delivered. Crowds gathered, and things were going great—until those in authority heard about it. They hauled the two missionaries to the municipal court, beat them, and threw them in jail.

Sitting in a dungeon, in chains, Paul and Silas did not wallow in misery. They did not harbor animosity toward their jailers. "How can God get the glory out of this situation?" was their response. As the clock struck midnight, they were praying and singing hymns. Their focus was not on the ones who had harmed them; rather, it was on God.

> Suddenly there was a great earthquake, so that the foundations of the prison were shaken; and immediately all the doors were opened and everyone's chains were loosed. And the keeper of the prison, awaking from sleep and seeing the prison doors open, supposing the prisoners had fled, drew his sword and was about to kill himself. But Paul called with a loud voice, saying, "Do yourself no harm, for we are all here." . . . And [the jailer] brought them out and said, "Sirs, what must I do to be saved?" (Acts 16:26–28, 30)

When God entered the situation, he not only freed Paul and Silas but also used them to lead the jailer to Christ. Now, if Paul and Silas could praise God under those extraordinary conditions, should we not try to incorporate praise into our daily lives as well? God is there for us in our midnights, just as he was in the Philippian jail for them.

When our landlord's staff was being so uncooperative, I tried to keep my focus on God. I didn't get angry—which is what I would have done earlier in my ministry. I would have yelled and complained and forced a confrontation. Instead, I remained calm. I asked the church to pray for us and them. Then I let our lawyer handle the dispute. He went to court and settled it agreeably.

Then the lease came up for renewal, and there was an additional conflict. Again, I had to continue praising God and keep my focus on him rather than taking out my frustration on the landlord. God even led me to pray for his salvation. I followed the biblical injunction of going to your adversary, and although the meeting was difficult, it was productive. The landlord's attitude started to soften. He agreed not to raise our rent, and then he actually lowered it. Today we speak rather frequently and amicably; it's an entirely new relationship. God answers prayer!

It Is Well with My Soul

When peace, like a river, attendeth my way,
When sorrows like sea billows roll;
Whatever my lot, Thou hast taught me to say,
It is well, it is well with my soul.

Chorus:
It is well with my soul,
It is well, it is well with my soul.

Tho' Satan should buffet, tho' trials should come,
Let this blest assurance control,
That Christ has regarded my helpless estate,
And hath shed His own blood for my soul.

My sin—oh, the bliss of this glorious tho't:
My sin not in part, but the whole
Is nailed to the cross and I bear it no more,
Praise the Lord, praise the Lord, O my soul!

And, Lord, haste the day when my faith shall be sight,
The clouds be rolled back as a scroll,

The trump shall resound and the Lord shall descend,
"Even so," it is well with my soul.

Horatio G. Spafford, the author of this beloved hymn, was a successful Chicago businessman with five children. His only son died suddenly, then Spafford suffered a serious financial loss in the great Chicago fire of 1871. About a year later, the family planned to sail to England to help the well-known evangelist D. L. Moody in a crusade there. Delayed by business, Spafford sent his wife and four daughters ahead. Another vessel struck their ship and it quickly sank; all four girls perished.

On the long voyage across the Atlantic to meet up with his wife, who had miraculously survived, Spafford stood on the ship's deck for hours, reflecting on his loss. Images of waves buffeting the ship were still in his mind as he later wrote, "When sorrows like sea billows roll . . . it is well with my soul."

This dear brother endured an unimaginably painful "midnight hour" of the soul, but he still found a song to sing. Through God's grace, and with the hope that he would one day be reunited with his children in glory, he could say, "It is well with my soul." Is it well with yours?

If you want to live victoriously, learn to sing in the midnight hours of life. When you start praising God in the middle of difficult circumstances, he will begin to change the situation. But if you respond in anger, or if you remain stuck in the past, you will block the blessing God has in store for you. Don't block your blessing—that's the next stop on our journey as we discover we are too blessed to be stressed.

CHAPTER TEN

Don't Block Your Blessing

Three days?" I repeated, wondering what I would do without my car for that long. A neighborhood body shop had fixed a bent tire rim, but the car still wasn't driving right. So I had brought it back to the dealership for what was turning out to be more extensive service.

"Yes, ma'am, it'll take that long," the mechanic said. "That pothole you hit did some major damage to your car. We have to order a part from the manufacturer, and it needs a complete realignment."

By taking a shortcut and trying to get by with a "quick fix," I had placed my car in jeopardy. The entire balance system was off. Out of whack. It needed special attention and parts that only the manufacturer could supply. Otherwise, my car would be off the road for good.

Our lives can also get out of whack. We are mind, body, and spirit, and unless all three are functioning in balance, we can't operate properly. We need the touch of our Maker and Manufacturer to put us back in alignment. And for maximum performance we need periodic checkups and a regular maintenance plan.

When I left my car that day, the dealership provided me with a loaner, a replacement car to drive until the mechanics finished the repairs on mine. But in life, we can't get a loaner. We must take care of the original body God gave us.

The Bible says that the body is the temple of the Holy Spirit:

> Do you not know that your body is the temple of the Holy Spirit who is in you, whom you have from God, and you are not your own? For you were bought at a price; therefore glorify God in your body and in your spirit, which are God's. (1 Cor. 6:19–20)

How precious it is to think that the Holy Spirit honors us with his presence. But our "temple" must be able to receive and respect the gift.

Too many people are running around the city, dashing across the nation, or jetting about the world, completely out of sync. It is more than jet lag they are experiencing. It is a spirit lag. They have tried shortcuts and quick fixes—perhaps a drink, a man, a day off, a minivacation here and there—but what they need is to be realigned with God.

Spiritual Time Zones

When we travel nationally and internationally, we reset our watches as we cross from one time zone to another. I believe there are spiritual time zones as well as physical ones. In the spirit realm we also cross over from one zone to another, from the old life to the new. Crossing that spiritual zone necessitates an adjustment. It requires getting in step with the Holy Spirit. "Since we live by the Spirit," Paul wrote, "let us keep in step with the Spirit" (Gal. 5:25 NIV).

Keeping in step with the Spirit means synchronizing our spirits with God's Spirit. Have you ever seen the synchronized swimmers in the Olympics? They move with amazing precision, but they do it so gracefully that the synchronization appears almost effortless. That precision, however, is the result of spending hours upon hours practicing as a team and getting the feel for the routine until every swimmer knows each motion intuitively and instinctively.

Our relationship with God can become synchronized. It requires spending time with him and learning to be sensitive to the Holy Spirit. "In him we live and move and have our being," the Word says (Acts 17:28 NIV). When we begin to move in sync with God, we will not experience so much stress because our bodies and spirits will be in the same place at the same time, and they will be in step with the Spirit.

When that happens, we will learn how to be content no matter what the circumstances. That was the lesson the apostle Paul had learned. He wrote, "I have learned to be content whatever the circumstances. I know what it is to be in need, and I know what it is to have plenty. I have learned the secret of being content in any and every situation, whether well fed or hungry, whether living in plenty or in want" (Phil. 4:11–12 NIV).

Paul was content because he was in step with the Spirit. A wonderful, liberating freedom comes when you reach that state of contentment in Christ. That's the point where you realize that stress does not have to stress you out. Situations and circumstances—bad or good—can change. But God is the same yesterday, today, and forever. Get in sync with him. Learn to be content. You don't have to live on an emotional roller coaster. You can find stability and security, fulfillment and contentment, and perfect peace of mind in Christ.

Stress Busters

If you are moving so fast that your spirit can't keep up with your body, here are a few tips to help you cope with some of the most common sources of stress.

Traffic-Jam Stress Buster

Plan to leave a half hour earlier than usual to anticipate the unexpected. That way you won't become stressed out if there is an accident or traffic tie-up. If you're caught in traffic, do not curse. Say, "God, I thank you for slowing me down. If this is the time you need to speak to me, then let me have the ears to hear you."

Speech-Delivery Stress Buster

If you are asked to give a speech, be clear on the topic, the amount of time allowed, and what the group is hoping will happen as a result of your speech.

Do not wait until the week before the event to do your research. Begin immediately so that you can use the last few days for practicing and rehearsing your speech.

Do not have too many critics giving you advice. Allow God's Spirit to bring to the surface what you already know. You can do it!

Family-Pressure Stress Buster

If family members are causing you stress, explain that you are working on a project or commitment for a little while and need some time alone. (You are the project/commitment, so this is not a lie.) Take the time and space you need. You will be surprised how fast others will get over it.

Reaction-to-the-Situation Stress Buster

Do not overeat. Do not take out a cigarette. Do not have a drink. Replace any or all of these behaviors with a short prayer: "Lord, help me."

Next, take a bath or go for a walk. Try to deal with this without crutches. Do not call someone. Find the strength God has placed within you. Say, "I can do all things through Christ who strengthens me" (Phil. 4:13).

Now pray again, this time a little longer. Use your own words to speak with God. After you have vented, thank God for listening.

End-of-a-Rough-Day Stress Buster

Write in your diary what you are feeling. If it is nice outside, take a long walk to unwind. If there is a park near your home, go outdoors and enjoy nature. Sit on a bench and study a tree. Find a bird and hear it sing. Look for God everywhere.

Can't-Keep-Up-with-the-Kids Stress Buster

Find a reputable baby-sitter, if you do not have a family support system, and pay her. Go out for breakfast, lunch, or dinner, or even a night on the town. You do not have to go with anyone. You will be surprised how much you will enjoy just being alone.

How-to-Get-Through-Life Stress Buster

Learn to pray without ceasing: "Rejoice always, pray without ceasing, in everything give thanks; for this is the will of God in Christ Jesus for you" (1 Thess. 5:16–18).

Get out of God's Way

Blessings, then, are gifts of God to help us align our bodies, minds, and spirits. How do we make these blessings a way of life? First we get in sync with God by spending time with him. Next we ask for specific blessings, and then we get out of God's way. Don't block your blessing!

Be specific in your prayer life. When you are a child, it's okay to pray, "God bless Mommy, and God bless me." As an adult, you need to state your case more clearly. A woman in my church was praying generally for God's blessing. When she finally started praying, "Lord, I need a job," she got one.

It's true that God already knows what you need before you ask. Prayer is for your benefit. It helps you clarify your needs and wants. Through prayer you align your desires with God's desires. James stated, "You do not have, because you do not ask

God. When you ask, you do not receive, because you ask with wrong motives, that you may spend what you get on your pleasures" (4:2–3 NIV).

Is there something you need today that you have not asked God for? When you do not ask, you are blocking your blessing. And when you ask, you must believe that God hears you and answers prayer. If you worry, why pray? And if you pray, why worry? Life is a faith journey. "We walk by faith, not by sight," according to the Bible (2 Cor. 5:7).

It's time to tell you how I met my wonderful husband. It happened when I learned to quit blocking my blessing. In my late twenties and early thirties, I went through a series of bad relationships. Family was always important to me, and I believed it was God's will for me to be married and have children. So I was out there looking and praying for Mr. Right. But I was attracting the wrong men into my life.

The final straw came in December 1990. I was dating a minister in another state, and I knew the relationship was not really working. I felt that I was giving 200 percent and getting back about 30 percent. But when he invited me to attend his installation as new pastor of a church, I made the trip, still hoping the relationship could be saved. When I arrived, however, I discovered that he had also invited his *other* girlfriend—someone I knew nothing about, of course—and she sat with his family during the service.

This is so rude, I kept thinking. I obviously didn't get much out of the sermon. On the way back to New York, I decided, *Enough already. I will not put myself under this kind of stress. And I will not start the New Year on an emotional roller coaster.*

Over the holidays I began to realize that God had blessed me, and he would not put me through the upheaval that some of these men had brought into my life. Then in early January a woman in my congregation came up to me after one of our lunch-hour services. I had been very public with my desire to get married and had often joked about it from the pulpit.

"You want a husband?" she said. "Go on a fast for a month. That's how I got my man."

"Did you get a good one?" I asked.

"He's the best man I could ever have. Try it," she urged me. "God really works."

Sometimes the pastor gets very good suggestions from the congregation. I thought about what this member said and decided to follow her advice.

Now fasting, which is abstaining from food and earnestly praying for a period of time, is not really my gift. I love to eat, and I knew fasting would be difficult. But my spirit said that this was the right thing to do. So I started a fast, and I began praying, "Lord, if I'm going to remain single, help me to deal with it. And if I'm supposed to be married, then please send the right man into my life. Because I will not accept anything less than the best any longer."

My thirty-day period of fasting and prayer, which turned out to be a blessed experience in itself, happened to coincide with Lent, the season of preparation for Easter. On the Monday of Holy Week, I went to Convent Avenue Baptist Church to hear Dr. Gardner Taylor, a popular preacher in New York. Dr. Taylor is called "the dean of black preachers" in the United States, and ministers from all over come to hear his Easter messages.

After the service I was planning to have dinner with a sister-friend. As I met up with her in the vestibule of the beautiful church in Harlem, I noticed a man who was duplicating cassette tapes of the service. *He sure is handsome,* I thought.

My friend had been an associate minister of that church, so I asked her, "Do you know who that man is?"

"That's Ron Cook," she said. "And I think he's single. Want me to introduce you?"

"No, no, no. It wouldn't be cool for a minister to appear to be hitting on somebody!" I laughed. But she could tell I was interested.

"Well, what if I invite him to have dessert with us?"

"Yeah, that's okay," I said. I was impressed at how smoothly she slipped over and asked him to meet us. Nobody suspected that I really was hitting on this man.

When Ron joined us at the restaurant, we instantly connected. I know it sounds corny, but it truly was love at first sight.

"I've always wanted to meet you," Ron said after we had ordered dessert. "In fact, I've wanted to take you out, but I didn't know how to go about asking the "reverend doctor" for a date. I thought you were unapproachable."

Suddenly I wished my sister-friend would make a trip to the ladies' room. She finally caught on and excused herself. The sparks really started flying, and Ron and I knew we wanted to spend some time alone.

"I've got a community board meeting in a couple of hours," Ron said.

"I could drive you there and we could talk for a while," I said. He agreed.

When my friend returned, we quickly paid the bill and then dropped her off at the church, where she had left her car. Ron and I drove to the neighborhood where his meeting would be held, and we had about an hour and a half to spend getting to know each other. We sat inside my car in front of a Kentucky Fried Chicken on 125th Street in Harlem. There was nothing at all romantic about the setting—we were under an elevated train, in front of a fast-food restaurant—but we were captivated by each other.

We made small talk for a few minutes, and then Ron said, "You know, I've been praying for a woman in my life. I've just spent the last month seriously praying that God would send me the right wife."

I nearly jumped out of my skin. I had just spent the last month praying for the right spouse.

"I'm ready to be married," he said, "but I don't want to marry just anyone. There has to be a spiritual connection. I want a woman who really knows the Lord."

The brother is reading my mind, I was thinking. I was almost afraid.

Ron kept talking, and even though there was a lot of chemistry between us, he was not flirtatious. It was obvious that he was a very sensitive, spiritual man who had really been praying about marrying a godly woman.

"If you are the gift God has sent me," he said, "I will be the best steward over this gift that the Lord could ever have." Everything he said resonated with my spirit. I didn't know whether to cry or shout or laugh, but I was pretty sure God was doing something incredible in my life.

"Suzan, I think we should both go to the Lord and ask him if we're the right ones for each other. And I won't even date you unless you get a confirmation from God that it's okay."

"That's a good idea," I said. "I'm ready to be married, too, but I don't want to rush into anything. I've also been fasting and praying for the Lord to send the right man into my life. And I'm not going to settle for less than God's best for me."

We agreed to pray for two or three days before we decided whether to see each other again. That was on a Monday, and on Wednesday Ron called me.

"What did God say?" he asked.

"I believe it's going to be okay," I answered. So we started dating.

A Blessing of Spiritual Strength

Ron and I started seeing each other during my seventh year at Mariners' Temple, and I was going through one of the most stressful periods of my ministerial career. The church was thriving financially as well as spiritually, but a handful of men in the church had decided that they would not follow a woman's leadership. They were openly rude and disrespectful to me. I was hurting, and the congregation was confused.

Ron came into my life at the height of the crisis. By that point I was so stressed out that I couldn't even pray about it anymore. Ron began to pray for me and with me. "I will take this to the Lord," he said. "I'm going to fast for you. But the one thing you cannot do is to run from this situation.

"You're like the prophet Elijah, who ran into the cave after his confrontation with the wicked Jezebel. God is telling you to come out of the cave, Suzan. You have to stand as God's prophet. You've done nothing wrong, so stand firm. This will soon be over. God will prevail."

Never in my life had anyone talked to me quite like that. I had always been showered with love by my family, and I always had their support. But Ron gave me more than love and support; he brought a spiritual strength that sustained me and fortified me.

About six weeks later there was a breakthrough, and God did prevail. Because of various incidents in their personal lives, the men who were making trouble left the church. Also, the congregation finally rose up and said, "We're standing with the pastor."

It was also a breakthrough in my relationship with Ron. I realized that if this man could sit with me through this terrible time in my life, then he certainly would be there for me in the good times.

So that's how I met my husband, when I quit blocking my blessing. I quit looking for Mr. Right and told God that *he* would have to bring my husband into my life—I was going to have God's man for me or no man at all.

And let me tell you: God's best is worth waiting for. *Can I get a witness?*

Singing in a Strange Land

Following the strategies I've recommended—getting in sync with God and not blocking your blessing—will help you reduce the stress in your life. But they won't eliminate stress entirely.

As I've said, our goal is to get to the point, physically, spiritually, and emotionally, where stress does not stress us out. I have also talked about learning to be content whatever our circumstances. Sometimes our circumstances can be quite difficult, even when we have gotten rid of as much of the stress as we can.

So what do we do when we find ourselves living in a "strange land"? We learn to sing.

The analogy I wish to make here is from Psalm 137. It's a psalm that describes the captivity of the Jewish people in Babylon. When their captors demanded that they sing, the captives asked, "How shall we sing the LORD's song in a strange land?" (v. 4 KJV).

His Eye Is on the Sparrow

Why should I feel discouraged, why should the
   shadows come,
Why should my heart be lonely, and long for heav'n
   and home,
When Jesus is my portion? My constant Friend is He;
His eye is on the sparrow, and I know He watches me;
His eye is on the sparrow, and I know He watches me;

Chorus:
I sing because I'm happy, I sing because I'm free,
For His eye is on the sparrow, and I know He watches me.

This song, penned by Civilla Martin in 1904, became the signature tune of the legendary Ethel Waters. Acclaimed by theater critics as one of the top-ranking dramatic actresses in America, Miss Waters sang "His Eye Is on the Sparrow" during the second act of the Broadway hit *The Member of the Wedding*—for 501 straight performances. She included the song in every one of her concerts thereafter.

Ethel Waters learned to "sing in a strange land." She was born to a twelve-year-old black girl who had been raped by a white boy. As a child, she attended church and learned to love Jesus. That's also where she learned to sing "Sparrow." "That song was the marrow in my bones," she wrote in her autobiography.[1] But she walked away from church, and away from her Lord, as a teenager. In 1957, when she was sixty-one, Ethel Waters returned to Christ through the ministry of Billy Graham. She quit the theater, canceled her club dates, and began thrilling crusade audiences across America with her eloquent, exquisite voice.

Many women feel they are in a strange land. Their particular strange land could be a rough marriage, an unexpected divorce, a child's death, the passing of a parent, or a job transition. Corporate women in high positions often feel they are on "foreign soil." Many minority women have had to learn how to perform, to rise to the occasion, in a strange land. They went to school and prepared for certain careers only to find those doors closed to them. Women in ministry have an especially tough time trying to find a place they can do what they believe God has called them to do.

Being in a strange land can extract a high price. It is not conducive to good health. Many women face devastating stress-related illnesses such as depression, sleep deprivation, and eating disorders. One of the reasons I do the Too Blessed to Be Stressed workshops is to teach women about God, so that when they are in a strange land they will have a power source on whom they can draw.

Women who learn to sing in the midst of strange surroundings are the ones who succeed in the Lord. Success in the Lord is demonstrated by faithfulness. Be faithful as you sing, but make sure it is the Lord's song that you sing. Learn to love God with all your heart, mind, and strength.

One of his followers once asked Jesus what the greatest commandment was.

"The most important one," answered Jesus, "is this: 'Hear, O Israel, the Lord our God, the Lord is one. Love the Lord your God with all your heart and with all your soul and with all your mind and with all your strength.'" (Mark 12:29–30 NIV)

Spend enough time with God to fall in love with him. Call upon his name frequently. You will find yourself singing even without music, and a heavenly choir will join your spirit in an orchestration that only God can compose.

Learning to sing God's song in a strange land will help you develop holding-on power, which is the final stop on our journey to discovering that we are too blessed to be stressed.

CHAPTER ELEVEN

Sisterstrength

O ne of the ironies of life is that joy and sorrow sometimes arrive simultaneously. That happened to me in the summer of 1991 when I became engaged to Ron.

We had been dating about four months when Ron came with me one weekend to my family's vacation home. Once we had gotten settled in, he asked my mother, "Could I please have a word with you, Mrs. Johnson?"

My heart almost stopped. He was about to ask my mother for my hand in marriage.

This is the moment I've been waiting for all my life, I thought. *Now it's happening, and I don't think I can handle it.*

I flew upstairs to be with my favorite aunt and uncle while Ron talked to my mother. I could not sit still.

"Why are you pacing the floor, Baby?" Uncle Cyrus asked.

"I'm just restless. I always need to move around after riding in the car for a while."

"What's Ron up to?" Aunt Katherine had a gleam in her eye. She knew something was going on.

"He's just talking to Mom," I said.

"Well now, I wonder what those two will find to talk about," Aunt Katherine said. She couldn't suppress a laugh.

I couldn't keep anything from Aunt Katherine. She was my closest aunt and my confidante. "He's asking for my mother's blessing on our marriage," I said.

"Honey, sit down before you wear the carpet out. And tell me all about it."

We chatted and giggled about the conversation going on downstairs. It was appropriate that Aunt Katherine was with me for this life-changing moment. I had spent so many happy times with this wonderful woman. When I landed my first job in television, I lived with her and Uncle Cyrus in Washington, D.C., until I could afford to get my own apartment. She had co-signed my application for my first credit card. When I moved back to New York, I still spent frequent weekends with them in Washington. Aunt Katherine loved to pamper me, and I loved letting her do it.

"Why is this taking so long?" I started pacing again. "I'm getting worried. It's been nearly an hour."

Finally I heard my mother's voice. "Suzan, please come downstairs."

This is it, I told myself. *Stay cool.*

When I reached the foot of the stairs, Mom was standing there beside Ron. "I've had a long talk with Ron," she said. "I believe he is God's choice for your life, Suzan. I give you my blessing."

I whooped for joy. We called for Aunt Katherine and Uncle Cyrus to come downstairs, and we officially announced our engagement to them. They gave their blessing as well, and we all went out to celebrate.

"This is a good one, Suzan. Don't lose him." Aunt Katherine laughed and joked with me at the restaurant. She was so excited for me, and we talked about how she would help me plan the wedding. She knew I was a spoiled brat, so she kept preaching to me, "Be good to Ron. He's a good man. You'd better treat him right."

Those were some of the last words Aunt Katherine ever spoke to me. On their trip back to Washington, she was killed in a car crash.

I would have felt keenly the loss of Aunt Katherine no matter when it happened. But losing her just as I was planning one of the most important events of my life made it even more painful. I simply could not imagine a special occasion in my life without her. She had been there for swim meets, piano recitals, and every graduation from kindergarten through college.

Suddenly I plunged from the heights of joy, planning my dream wedding, to the depths of sorrow, planning a funeral for one of the people I loved most in all the world.

A part of me was still grieving on my wedding day four months later. Afterward I caught myself looking for her in our wedding photos; it didn't seem possible that she wasn't there. And I missed her again when I was pregnant with my first child. I could imagine visiting Aunt Katherine when I felt the need for pampering.

What do you do when joy and sorrow show up on your doorstep on the same day? How do you keep the pieces together when you're as broken as Humpty-Dumpty and the whole wall is tumbling down on top of you?

You may be coping with the loss of a loved one right now. Perhaps that loss is not the result of death, but a painful separation or transition. Perhaps a marriage you truly felt was made in heaven dissolved unexpectedly. Or perhaps an aging parent has become ill and needs constant attention, more than you ever imagined you would have to give.

When you're facing emotional trauma, you may feel like giving up. Often it's not a single event that dismays you, but the cumulative effect of many stressful situations. There have been many days I wanted to "hang up my sneakers," as the basketball players say. I felt I had had enough, and I was tempted to call it quits.

You've had those days, too, haven't you? A day when the very person you tried to help turns around and leads an attack against you. A day when you get laid off your job and you were already sinking financially. Or you come home and find that the loved one who supposedly "kicked the habit" hasn't even come close. Circumstances you didn't ask for, and certainly didn't want, have combined to sap your strength and bruise your spirit.

Life is full of twists and turns and tragedies. We have good days and bad days, days that are truly rough, and days that we think we'll never live through. How do we find the strength to hold on? Two biblical characters give us some clues.

Holding-On Power

Perhaps you're familiar with the story of Ruth and Naomi. These two biblical she-roes are good examples of what I call holding-on power, the power we need to face whatever life hands us.

Naomi and Ruth were widows. At that point in history women were defined by the men in their lives. Away from their homeland and bereft of their husbands, they found strength in each other and in God. This tragedy-to-triumph story shows how two women developed a wonderful intimacy and learned to befriend each other through difficult times.

Naomi was the older, seasoned woman who should have been enjoying her golden years. A recession had driven Naomi and her husband of many years from their home, Bethlehem in Judah, to the country of Moab. Together with their two sons, they ventured out with hope and faith in God's provision. They lived for a while in Moab as an intact family, but before they could return to their homeland, Naomi's husband died.

Ruth, the protagonist of the story, was Naomi's daughter-in-law. She was a young woman who should have been enjoying her new marriage and starting a family, but her husband died prematurely. In fact, both of Naomi's sons died in quick succession, leaving her destitute. In Bible times, a widow was in a precarious position economically. Widows with no sons to care for them often died in bitter poverty.

Ruth and Orpah, Naomi's other daughter-in-law, were young enough to remarry—but what would Naomi do? Would her daughters-in-law want to care for an aged woman once they had new families of their own? When Naomi heard that the financial picture in Judah had improved, she decided to return to her homeland. *At least there*, she thought, *I will die among friends.*

Orpah wept and kissed her mother-in-law as Naomi set out on her journey. "But Ruth clung to her," the Bible says (Ruth 1:14). A spiritual enterprise had been established between Naomi and Ruth. They were bound to each other not only by family ties and circumstances, but also by God. Ruth vowed to return with Naomi, even though she was free to remain in Moab, the only home she had ever known.

In one of the most moving passages in Scripture, Ruth announced her decision to Naomi:

> Entreat me not to leave you,
> Or to turn back from following after you;
> For wherever you go, I will go;
> And wherever you lodge, I will lodge;
> Your people shall be my people,
> And your God, my God.
> Where you die, I will die,
> And there will I be buried.
> The LORD do so to me, and more also,
> If anything but death parts you and me. (Ruth 1:16–17)

Ruth's words are so beautiful, and express such a deep bond of love, that many couples have used these verses as part of their wedding vows. But the context here is not romantic love. These were not whispered "sweet nothings" from an overflowing heart. No, these were words of commitment spoken from the depth of Ruth's soul.

Naomi and Ruth began their arduous journey to Bethlehem on a happy note of companionship. As they traveled, however, the grief and devastation of her losses so overwhelmed Naomi that when she arrived home, she could not even rejoice. Her friends, who had not seen her for at least ten years, were excited. "Is it really Naomi?" they asked.

In her deepening depression, Naomi refused to be called by her own name. "Do not call me Naomi," she said. "Call me Mara, for the Almighty has dealt very bitterly with me" (Ruth 1:20).

It was a desperate moment. Naomi was about to give up. She was in a broken place in her life, the kind of place that leaves us feeling raw and vulnerable. The feeling of brokenness is not one that we covet, but brokenness can also lead to blessedness.

Ruth was the blessing for Naomi during that difficult time. As we mature as Christians, we must learn to see and appreciate the blessing at hand. We must develop holding-on power. And holding on means grabbing the blessing that is within our reach.

Naomi's faithful daughter-in-law reminded her of the God she had called upon and had spoken about when things were going well in her life. That same God would also be there for them when things were rough. So Naomi's earlier testimony about God became her breakthrough from God.

That is why it is so important to know God before the storms and trials of life come, for sometimes all it takes is a gentle reminder of what is already inside your spirit. Naomi needed Ruth's support and strength, but Naomi's holding-on power came from what she had already internalized.

God is there for us through all kinds of weather. He is our shelter in the time of storm, "a very present help in trouble" (Ps. 46:1). Naomi was blessed by Ruth's pledge not to leave her. How much more are we blessed by God's promise never to forsake us: "He is the One who goes before you. He will be with you, He will not leave you nor forsake you; do not fear nor be dismayed" (Deut. 31:8).

A Shelter in the Time of Storm

If you need holding-on power, find a sister-friend and join
your voices in this old hymn of the church. If you know the
tune, sing it. If not, read it out loud. Jesus will lift your spirits.

> The Lord's our Rock, in Him we hide,
> A shelter in the time of storm;
> Secure whatever ill betide,
> A shelter in the time of storm.
>
> Chorus:
> Oh, Jesus is a Rock in a weary land,
> A weary land, a weary land;
> Oh, Jesus is a Rock in a weary land,
> A shelter in the time of storm.
>
> O Rock divine, O Refuge dear,
> A shelter in the time of storm;
> Be Thou our helper ever near,
> A shelter in the time of storm.

This hymn was written in 1869 by Vernon J. Charlesworth,
a British pastor. Fishermen who trolled the north coast of England often sang it as they sailed into harbor in stormy weather.

Ira D. Sankey, the musician who traveled with the great
revivalist Dwight L. Moody, wrote the tune. At the time, many
Christians were opposed to the rhythmic gospel music Sankey
introduced. His music doesn't have much "soul" by today's
standards, but I still love the words. The Lord is my Rock!

Ruth reminded Naomi to stir up the faith within her. She was
not only a daughter-in-law; she was also a sister-friend. Like
Naomi, we may face situations where we want to give up. But

when we belong to Christ, we will have the strength we need inside us at the time we need it the most. Sometimes all we need is a sister-friend to remind us.

Sisterstrength

Ruth and Naomi illustrate what I call *sisterstrength*, the strength that comes from a support system of sister-friends who will stand with you through all kinds of weather. Sisterstrength comes from women who will affirm you, who will provide the outer strength that will connect with your inner strength, no matter what the circumstances.

I taught a class at my high school alma mater two years ago. One of the students, a mature senior, described her relationship with her best friend. She said, "We are two halves who, when we are together, make a whole." That's sisterstrength.

Life has its storms, but the strong will survive. I have experienced storms, hurricanes, and even tornadoes, figuratively speaking, yet I have held on with the support of my sister-friends.

Sisterstrength is directly tied into another word I coined, *sistertherapy*. By that I mean the sisterly love and understanding shared between two women who care about each other.

I used both of these terms once in addressing a group of female mayors who had come to a conference in New York. As I described the spiritual and sisterly compatibility of Ruth and Naomi, they nodded their heads and clapped their hands in support of what I said. Many of them could definitely relate to either having been there for another woman or having another woman be there for them.

Many pastors and church leaders ask if I can be there for women on their staff who are new in the ministry and may need coaching from a sister-friend. I say yes as often as I am able because I understand the need for sisterstrength and sistertherapy.

I also remember what it was like when I got my start in the church world. In pastoral ministry, there are far fewer role models for women than for men. I had to learn many lessons by trial and error, so sharing my experiences with other women can help them leapfrog some of the problem areas.

For example, I noticed that most men changed their shirts after preaching, but the few female preachers I knew didn't change clothes afterward. We would take off our robes and go out in the cold air and then wonder why we were hoarse. When you preach vigorously, it's like running a five-mile race. The men were not changing shirts because of pride in their appearance or an interest in personal hygiene. They did it so they wouldn't get sick. When you perspire, your pores open up; putting on dry clothing closes them, and that protects you from getting a cold or sore throat.

One time I noticed that my mentor, Pastor Wells, wore special socks when he preached. "They keep me from getting varicose veins," he told me. So I started wearing support hose, and they made a big difference. When I don't wear them, I feel my legs throbbing after I preach.

These are just two lessons I have passed along to other women. I have been blessed to mentor seven women, my "spiritual daughters" in the faith, as they prepared for and entered the ranks of ministry. We spent a lot of time together sharing, most of it at an early morning session I designated as the Prophet's Hour.

We would meet at the church an hour before anyone else arrived. It was our special time to share, to vent, to learn, and to prepare to deliver a prophetic word to our world. Some days someone would be feeling, like Naomi, that God was dealing bitterly with her. Other times we would celebrate victories and reflect on how much they had grown. We got on each other's nerves sometimes—they often thought I was too strict and rigid, and I thought they were too lax in some areas—but we developed a deep love for one another during those early morning hours.

Usually I was the one helping them, but they also helped me when I needed it. They were my sisterstrength, the ones who stood beside me as Mariners' Temple grew to a congregation of one thousand people, and my sistertherapy, the ones who saw me through my burnout.

These very special women deserve to have an entire book written about them, but I will at least mention them briefly here. The ones who were with me the longest are Henrietta Carter, Carolyn Holloway, Sheila Grimes, and Valerie Eley. Henrietta and Carolyn came from New York Theological Seminary and were the first two female students to do their field placement work with me at Mariners'. Sheila and Valerie were members of Mariners' whom God called into the pastorate through my ministry. Mariners' Temple became a national pulpit while I was there, and pastors from across the country wanted to see our church firsthand. We set a standard for excellence in ministry, and people had their eyes on this team of black women in New York.

A former elementary school teacher of the year in New York City, Henrietta served as our Christian education director and later as assistant pastor of Mariners'. She was the one who kept the church going while I spent a year at the White House. And when I eventually left Mariners', Henrietta served as interim pastor.

Carolyn now pastors her own congregation, DeWitt Reformed Church, about twenty blocks from Mariners' Temple. She became the second black woman pastor in the Reformed denomination. And Carolyn, who used to look at me funny when I called a meeting for 7:30 A.M., is in her office quite early these days. She now holds her own Prophet's Hour, mentoring other women in ministry.

Sheila, the first woman to be called into the ministry under my leadership, is a true example of success. She had married and had children while she was still quite young, So while Sheila was serving as our minister of administration, and being a mother to four children, she also enrolled in college. She finished her bachelor's degree, and she is now in seminary studying for her Master of Divinity.

When Valerie steps to the microphone and sings a gospel song, every heart is touched. She was a Broadway singer when she started attending our lunch-hour service at Mariners'. She later joined the church, and God called her into the ministry. At first she wanted to do only music ministry, but I encouraged her to develop her other gifts. An intellectual as well as an artist, Valerie is now at Howard University Divinity School, working on her doctorate in patristics and studying the African contributions to the Bible and the early church.

The Lord greatly used this team of women to do something spectacular at Mariners' Temple. Occasionally someone would comment, "There are no men in leadership here. Shouldn't there be more balance?"

I would reply, "Nobody ever questions it when there are no women in leadership at a particular church. What's the difference? These are the people God sent us, so these are the people we're going to use."

Over the years, other women came into the Prophet's Hour. Gladys Lawrence, another terrific singer, is now in North Carolina. Leatha Johnson is with Carolyn Holloway at DeWitt Reformed. And Annette Cox is at Bronx Christian Fellowship with me. Annette is from the corporate world, and she skillfully handles a lot of administrative work—the two of us now do the same work that seven staff members did at Mariners'.

I started out as the mentor, but these sister-friends, most of whom were already mothers, had the opportunity to mentor me through a very significant event: the birth of my first child. A pregnant pastor is a phenomenon that only other women could understand. Who else would know what morning sickness feels like in the pulpit?

I was sick for eight out of nine months while I was carrying Samuel, and not just in the mornings. Everything I ate came up. When I got sick in the pulpit, I would have the congregation sing a hymn, then I would go to the rest room, throw up, and come back. Most people had no idea what was going on. When one of our ushers, Patricia, learned I was pregnant and nauseated all the time, she started waiting offstage with some crackers and ginger ale. Eventually I learned which foods triggered the worst queasiness and quit having to leave the pulpit so often.

Samuel learned to love gospel music while he was still in the womb. We would be singing and praising the Lord, and it felt like Samuel was dancing along with the rest of us. But he really got excited when I preached. It was sometimes difficult to get out a clear word of God with a rambunctious boy inside me trying to play basketball.

The week before Samuel was born, I quit preaching. I finally was too uncomfortable going up and down the pulpit stairs. I think the congregation was relieved—I looked so pregnant that people were worried I was going to deliver in the pulpit.

My sister ministers demonstrated their love for me throughout my pregnancy and delivery in many ways. They generously made sure our nursery was fully supplied, knowing far better than I what all we would need. They organized a prayer vigil at the church while I was in labor. I had never been in the hospital before Samuel was born, so Carolyn even packed my overnight bag for me.

These women also helped me and the church handle the challenges presented by a pregnant pastor. Some of the issues that cropped up were humorous: What do you do when the robe you preach in is too tight because your breasts are so big? And some were serious: How do you persuade a church board to adopt a policy granting maternity leave for the pastor?

The sisterstrength I received from the women of the Prophet's Hour helped me hold on. How can you find the holding-on power you need to get through life? A lot of it depends on who is there to hold on to. Sometimes a sister-friend relationship already exists. Cherish it. At other times adversity may bring you to your sister–soul mate. The writer of Proverbs said, "A friend loves at all times, / And a brother is born for adversity" (17:17). I want you to know that verse is not just for the brothers—it's for the sisters too.

However or wherever sisterstrength presents itself, know that God's hand is in the middle of it. Just as I believe that God has a person's life partner and soul mate already handpicked, I believe that friends are also a divine gift. The story of Naomi and Ruth reminds us that even when life's circumstances are disabling, we should still hold on, trusting God to send those we need exactly when we need them. He will.

Affirmations

Often we need reminders of the spiritual lessons we are learning. I call these reminders affirmations because they affirm what God is doing in our lives. Affirmations are like spiritual sticky notes for the soul. These are the things I have told myself over and over until my mind finally connected with my spirit.

Some of these affirmations you will want to memorize. Others you may want to write out on note cards and put them where you will see them frequently throughout the day: on the refrigerator or bathroom mirror or baby's crib, on your desk or filing cabinet, on the dashboard of your car—okay, you'd better memorize that one or read it only when you're stopped at a traffic light!

- "I can do all things through Christ who strengthens me" (Phil. 4:13).
- I am God's woman. I am important to God.
- God has a plan for my life, and it is a good plan (Jer. 29:11).
- I am not God's stepchild. I am God's child.
- I am a joint heir with Jesus Christ (Rom. 8:17).
- Fun is permitted. I will enjoy life today.
- Jesus came to bring me abundant life (John 10:10).

- "Weeping may endure for a night, / But joy comes in the morning" (Ps. 30:5). Good morning, joy!
- I will not block my blessings. I will get out of God's way.
- "I will bless the LORD at all times; / His praise shall continually be in my mouth" (Ps. 34:1).
- I will be still and know God today (Ps. 46:10).
- Whatever it is, God is already working it out.
- I know where I'm going, and I'm going forward.
- I will enjoy each season of my life. It may be winter right now, but spring will surely come (Eccl. 3).
- Yes, I want to be made whole.
- I am complete in Christ (Col. 2:10).
- I am renewing my mind (Rom. 12:2).
- It's not hard to be there for a friend. I will do it.
- "A friend loves at all times, / And a [sister] is born for adversity" (Prov. 17:17).
- I need sisterstrength. I will give love and sisterstrength to the women I meet.
- I am too blessed to be stressed.

A Call from the White House

For a few months last year I had a "normal" life, coming home at six o'clock every day and enjoying quiet evenings with my family. Well, *quiet* is a relative term when you have two boys under five years old. *Can I get a witness?*

Late last spring I had a speaking engagement in Hyannis, Massachusetts. I had left a number with my staff where I could be reached in an emergency. I didn't expect to hear from them because I have a great staff and they can handle just about everything in my absence.

So I was surprised when I got a call from my office manager. I was even more surprised when she said, "The White House has been trying to reach you all night."

Immediately I returned the call of the man who was trying to contact me. He said, "The president has personally asked me to call you. He wants to know if you would consider being on an advisory board that would deal with race in America." He named a half dozen other people who were being considered. "The board will convene in the next couple of months and will work directly with the president."

"How was my name selected?" I asked him.

"President Clinton personally selected you. He's been watching you and feels you have a lot to offer."

I remembered the day I had met him as a White House fellow. "You're the Baptist preacher I've been hearing about," the president said as he shook my hand. That was the day he asked me to pray with him.

"I appreciate your call," I told the man from the White House. "May I get back to you tomorrow?"

When I hung up the phone, I screamed in excitement. I talked it over with Ron. I called my mother and brother back in New York. They all said, "You have to do it. It's the president calling. How many people ever get this kind of opportunity?"

It wasn't just the opportunity to work with the president, although I certainly considered that an honor. It was the opportunity to work on an issue that has always been at the forefront of my concern. Since my childhood days in Freedom School, I have looked for ways to get involved in justice issues. Racism is one of the most critical problems facing our nation, and I had been asked for my input. As I considered my decision, I concluded that God had been preparing me for just this kind of position.

I called the White House back the next morning and gave permission for my name to be put on the list of candidates. Then we went through a series of investigations, which always accompany a White House appointment. In June 1997 I was named as one of seven members of a national advisory board to be known as the President's Initiative on Race and Reconciliation.

A few days later the seven new board members were briefed by President Clinton in the Oval Office, and then a motorcade delivered us to *Air Force One* for a trip to the West Coast, where the president would announce the new initiative in his address to the University of California at San Diego. This Baptist preacher dined on spareribs—presidential spareribs served at thirty thousand feet, mind you—while consulting with the nation's chief executive on a major policy speech. *Hello, somebody!*

Advising the president on what he should say in his speech was both a heady and a humbling experience. But I realized that if God had placed me in that position, then I had a responsibility to serve.

So, as I've said, I enjoyed a few months of "normal" life before this latest adventure. Leaders are called to lead lives that, many times at least, are not normal. I may have to take some other things out of my life in order to add this new commitment. But that's a decision I was comfortable making.

As I finish this book, the pace is just beginning to pick up for the presidential advisory board. I don't know how much time and travel will be involved, but I know serving on it will consume a lot of my energy. However, my personal life is in order now, so I have more time and energy to give.

I also have a firm understanding of what it means to be too blessed to be stressed. And I hope you have learned that lesson as well, my sister-friend. *Can I get a witness?*

Notes

Chapter One
1. John Bartlett, *Familiar Quotations*, 15th ed. (Boston: Little, Brown, 1980), 823.

Chapter Three
1. W. L. Doughty, ed., *The Prayers of Susanna Wesley* (Grand Rapids, Mich.: Zondervan, 1984), 7–8.

Chapter Six
1. *The Words of Martin Luther King Jr., Selected by Coretta Scott King* (New York: New Market Press, 1983), 24.

Chapter Eight
1. Suzan Johnson Cook, ed., *Sister to Sister, Devotions for and from African American Women* (Judson Press: Valley Forge, 1995).
2. Albert Edward Bailey, *The Gospel in Hymns* (New York: Charles Scribner's Sons, 1950), 138.

Chapter Ten
1. Ethel Waters, *To Me It's Wonderful* (New York: Harper and Row, 1972), 11.

About the Author

Suzan D. Johnson Cook, D. Min., is one of seven people recently appointed by President Bill Clinton to serve with the President's Initiative on Race and Reconciliation and named by *Ebony* magazine as one of the top fifteen women in ministry in the nation. She is the organizer and senior pastor of the Bronx Christian Fellowship. Prior to this, she served for thirteen years as the senior pastor of the Mariners' Temple Baptist Chruch, the oldest American Baptist Church in New York City. There she hosted the "Hour of Power," a lunchtime service for government employees, stockbrokers, and other Manhattan employees. She was the first African-American woman elected senior pastor for the American Baptists, the first woman chaplain for the New York City Police Department, and the first woman officer of the historic Hampton University Ministers' Conference, the largest gathering of African-American clergy in the world.

She received a B.S. from Emerson College, an M.A. from Teachers College, Columbia University, an M.Div. from Union Theological Seminary, and a D.Min. from the United Theological Seminary. She is the editor of the internationally acclaimed best-seller *Sister to Sister: Devotions for and from African American Women* and coauthor of *Preaching in Two Voices*.

For booking information, please call or write:

Sujay Ministries, Inc.
PO Box 226
Peck Slip Station
New York, NY 10272-0226
(800) 318-9979